SCUBA LIFE SAVING

Albert Pierce

Produced by
The Royal Life Saving Society Canada

Published by
Leisure Press
Champaign, Illinois

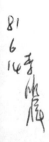

Typesetter: Attic Typesetting Inc.
Text Design: LeCamp Graphic Design
Cover Photo: Tom Stack/Tom Stack and Associates
Printed By: United Graphics, Inc.

ISBN: 0-88011-279-4

Scuba Life Saving was originally published by The Royal Life Saving Society
Canada (ISBN: 0-920326-23-4) and is available in Canada from the RLSSC.

Library of Congress Cataloging-in-Publication Data

Pierce, Albert.
   Scuba life saving.

    1. Scuba diving--Safety measures. 2. Scuba
diving--Accidents and injuries. 3. Life-saving.
I. Royal Life Saving Society Canada. II. Title.
GV840.S78P54 1986 797.2'3'0289 86-10308
ISBN 0-88011-279-4

Printed in the United States of America
10 9 8 7 6 5

Leisure Press
A Division of Human Kinetics Publishers, Inc.
Box 5076, Champaign, IL 61825-5076
1-800-747-4457

UK Office:
Human Kinetics Publishers (UK) Ltd.
P.O. Box 18
Rawdon, Leeds LS19 6TG
England
(0532) 504211

PREFACE

In spite of the many potential problems that may arise in scuba diving, it is really a very safe sport. Of the increasing millions in the United States and Canada who enjoy the thrill of gliding weightlessly through the fascinating and beautiful underwater world, very few are injured or killed. Much of the credit for the consistently low accident rate goes to the thousands of scuba instructors, assistants and divemasters who are dedicated to safe diving practices.

If you haven't yet participated in an actual rescue, the odds are that you will. Studies of diver rescue reports indicate that over 60% of the respondents have performed a rescue and in fact close to 20% were called upon to perform resuscitation.

Scuba diving is influenced by rapidly changing technology. Some rescue methods currently utilized will no doubt be revised because of the improvements in this technology. The purpose of this book is to describe the current situation and to stimulate thought, discussion, research, experimentation and practice.

This book is a compilation, consolidation and condensation of scuba lifesaving and self-rescue techniques furnished by you—diving physicians, authors, instructors, divemasters, scuba divers, snorklers and other aquatic enthusiasts.

I am indebted to Dennis Graver, who as Projects Director for the National Association of Underwater Instructors (NAUI), started me writing this book, and who, as Training Director for the Professional Association of Diving Instructors (PADI), continued to encourage and offer suggestions.

I am also indebted to Robert W. Smith, former Director of the YMCA Underwater Activities Program, who spearheaded the Scuba Lifesaving and Accident Management (SLAM) project. Many of the techniques described in this book were evaluated both in and out of the water during SLAM sessions. This project, funded by grants from the Council for National Cooperation in Aquatics (CNCA) and the National Oceanic and Atmospheric Administration (NOAA), resulted in a new chapter (Section 18 on Accident Management) in the revised second edition of the *NOAA Diving Manual,* and in the production of the booklet, *Scuba Lifesaving and Accident Management.* Besides myself, participants in the SLAM project at Key West were Warren Glaser, representing PADI, Larry Gibson of the World Life Saving, Jenny Brown-Pill of the Royal Life Saving Society Canada, Bob Orozco of the National YMCA Aquatic Program, Louise Priest, then Deputy National Director of the Red Cross Water Safety Program, Dr. Harry Heinitsh of the U.S. Army Medical Corps (Special Forces—Underwater Operations), and H. Clement Allen, co-author with Smith of *Scuba Lifesaving and Accident Management.*

Thanks to Stephen F. Hardick, editor of *Underwater Search and Recovery,* for arranging the voluminous Xeroxing, to Adele McCloskey for negotiating the typing of the manuscript, and to Jim Morrow for making it more readable.

Many thanks also to Hardick and to the following other distinguished divers for reviewing the manuscript and offering suggestions: the late Charles V. Brown, M.D., medical editor for *Skin Diver* and *NAUI News*; Bruce Bassett, Ph.D., President of Human Underwater Biology, Inc.; Robert Brandeberry, author of *Open Water Lifesaving Techniques for Divers*; Jocelyn Palm, Executive Director, Royal Life Saving Society Canada, author of *Alert: Aquatic Supervision in Action;* Peter R. Lynch, Ph.D., Temple University School of Medicine; Stephen G. Metcalf, PADI International Liaison Agent; Harry Heinitsh, M.D., Diving Medical Consultant for the YMCA Centre for Underwater Activities; Lou Fead, author of *Easy Diver,* and D. Lee Kvalnes, Ph.D., both of whom are members of the NAUI Board of Directors.

Drawings are by Jim Mitchell except as noted.

Finally, special thanks to Jocelyn Palm, Ed Bean, Jenny Brown-Pill, Art Penney, John Armstrong, Dave Linton, Gord Lemon, and Dave Addyman who provided the final edit and completed this project.

Albert L. Pierce
Author

FOREWORD

This book is a unique venture in cooperation among aquatic agencies in North America. Members of the Royal Life Saving Society Canada (RLSSC) have participated over the years in conferences on scuba diving and in the semi-annual conferences of the Council for National Cooperation in Aquatics (CNCA). The mutual respect and sharing of information among the aquatic personnel has produced many positive results. In one such exchange, the work of Al Pierce became known. His original intent was to publish his efforts through one of the U.S. agencies or organizations. The RLSSC initiated a scuba life saving program in 1976, called the Scuba Bronze. The RLSSC wanted a text and as it transpired CNCA needed a publisher for Al Pierce's book.

The complexity of preparing a text for scuba lifesaving training must not be underestimated. We take it for granted that every diver needs training in self-rescue and the rescue of others, but we dare not assume that an emergency will unfold in any standard format. Divers must succeed in developing the creative and resourceful attitude to which Al Pierce refers in his preface. Only then will they be able to respond appropriately when called upon in a real emergency.

The RLSSC acknowledges the efforts of both Dave Addyman and Jenny Brown-Pill in the development of the RLSSC Scuba Life Saving Program. The RLSSC is grateful to Al Pierce for gathering all the various details which are included in this text and pleased to provide this information to those who need it—the scuba enthusiasts.

Jocelyn Palm
Executive Director
The Royal Life Saving Society Canada

CONTENTS

CHAPTER 1

Scuba life saving is unique

As a diver, you depend on other divers to help you in emergencies and, if necessary, to save your life. You are also one of those "other" divers. Whenever you dive, you accept a responsibility to be alert, to recognize problems early, and to attempt to avoid them.

The odds are that you will be required to make a rescue. In a study on Buddy Diving, Lou Fead found that his respondents had these experiences with actual victims:

- over 60% had rescued a fellow diver
- almost 60% had shared air
- almost 60% had towed another diver
- almost 20% had given air mouth-to-mouth
- almost 10% had used cardiopulmonary resuscitation (CPR)

Any diver may have to make a rescue on the next dive. Scuba life saving techniques should be taught and discussed at all levels of scuba training, from basic classes and dive club programs to the most advanced workshops.

It is environment and equipment that make scuba life saving unique. The victim may be: underwater or ice, in crashing surf, high waves, strong currents or very cold water, surrounded by rough coral, jagged wrecks, or tangles of fish net or kelp. The diver in difficulty could be disoriented by featureless bottoms, blinding silt, dark caves, or changes in pressure. There may be dangerous life above or below, including the most dangerous, the unthinking scuba diver.

Scuba equipment could hamper a rescue.

The suit and buoyancy compensator (BC) restrict both movement and breathing. The tank, backpack and weight belt change the diver's balance while the mask may give tunnel vision. Add the regulator, watch, depth gauge, snorkel, whistle, knife, light, compass, and so on, and a diver may feel as mobile as an overdecorated Christmas tree.

That heavy, bulky equipment can also help in making rescues. But it must be used correctly and be properly maintained.

The most obvious rescue advantage is the ability to breathe underwater, but gear has other major assets. The wet or dry suit allows a diver to function in cold water which would debilitate an unprotected person in minutes. Weights and BC permit full control of buoyancy. A sharp knife allows a diver to cut entanglements, such as fish line or kelp. A light can help to signal a buddy or locate a victim in murky water. Mask and snorkel permit rapid location of an underwater victim. Fins provide extra power for a tow or height at the surface for efficient rescue breathing.

Scuba gear can help, but remember that all equipment has limits. Almost any piece of gear may be disabled when needed, or be knocked away during a rescue, particularly if the victim is panicked.

Prepare for a rescue situation

Prevent accidents

It is always better—and easier—to prevent an accident than to correct its effects. Some effects, such as permanent injury or death, can never be corrected. Others may involve years of rehabilitation with intense pain and enormous medical bills.

Practice rescue skills

Your rescue skills grow each time you practice them. Overlearn each skill until it becomes automatic, and practice to keep it that way. In a rescue, your mind should be on *what* to do, not trying to recall *how* to do it.

Recognize problems

Every day accident victims die in the presence of others who could have helped if only they had recognized the problem. Divers must train their senses to see, hear or feel problems as they develop. Be aware of anything that could affect you or those with you.

Learn victim recognition

Victims may be rational, passive, or panicky. The rational victim knows he is in trouble, but is not overwhelmed by it. This victim can be approached safely and can often help in the rescue.

The passive victim is effectively unconscious and may be non-breathing. This person cannot grab a float, a line, or you. He requires immediate assistance.

The panic-stricken victim may not be safe to approach. His thoughts all center on getting air for himself. On the surface, he may climb onto your head, knock away your mask and regulator and sink you in his frantic attempt to get air.

General rescue principles

No two rescues will ever be exactly alike. There are always unpredictable factors in any situation; the environment, equipment, the victim, the rescuer. However, most rescues involve certain general principles. Knowing

Fig. 1-1

A panicky victim may sink you to get air.

these principles make a rescue easier, faster, safer, and more successful.

- **Stop and think**

  Whoever is in trouble—you or someone else—*stop and think before you act*! Too many would-be heroes have drowned along with the victim, or in many cases *instead* of the victim, by rushing into danger without considering other, safer methods. Many have panicked and drowned needlessly. Most scuba emergencies don't require instantaneous action. Take a few seconds to think!

- **Know your limits**

  Unless you possess the skills to make the rescue safely do not attempt it. Call for help or wait until the situation is safer.

  Pace yourself. Save your energy for dealing with the victim, for towing him to safety, and for unforeseen circumstances. At any point in the rescue, you should be able to let go and save yourself.

- **Use the least hazardous method**

  Whenever they are available, use lines, floats, boards, or boats. Sometimes you don't even have to get wet.

Remember that *you* are the most important person in any rescue attempt. If you are injured, you may not be able to save yourself, much less the victim.

- **Enlist help**

  Obtain help from all possible sources. Ask the victim to help if he can.

  Call for help from others, but do not wait for them unless you would put yourself in danger, or could not help, by acting alone.

  Once you have stabilized the situation, keep calling or signalling for help. Don't give up, even if you feel completely alone. Someone may get the message and respond.

- **Maintain visual contact**

  Someone should observe the victim continuously especially a victim on the surface. The diver might sink or his condition may change. Maintain visual contact while swimming or boating towards the victim. In rough water where waves block your vision, spotters in the boat or on shore should point and shout directions.

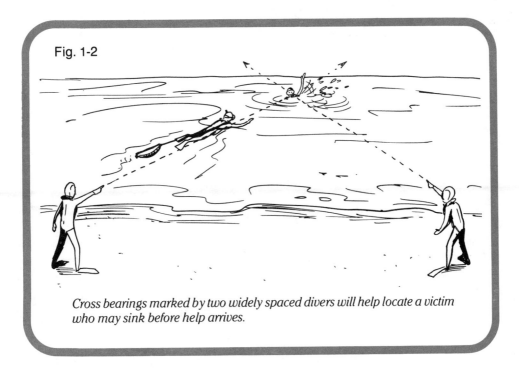

Fig. 1-2

Cross bearings marked by two widely spaced divers will help locate a victim who may sink before help arrives.

- **Establish respiration**
  An unconscious, non-breathing victim must get air immediately. Begin rescue breathing as soon as the victim's face is above water.

  An out-of-air victim who is still conscious needs immediate access to air. The source may be: an underwater supply from a pony bottle, octopus rig, buoyancy compensator, buddy breathing, from the expansion of air during ascent, or air above the surface.

- **Establish buoyancy**
  A panicky victim will usually calm down as soon as he can rest and breathe easily.

  Give him something that floats or help him inflate his buoyancy compensator, drop his weights, or lie on his back.

- **Continually assess the situation**
  The environment, equipment, buoyancy, victim's behavior, etc. can change rapidly. Be alert to possible changes and alter your technique if necessary in order to keep the rescue as safe and effective as possible.

- **Account for the victim's buddy**
  When one diver is in trouble, the buddy might be in worse trouble. Until you can account for the buddy, assume there are two victims. If possible, without minimizing help for the known victim, determine the buddy's identity and status. The rescue is not over until all are accounted for.

- **Follow up**
  At the conclusion of the rescue, ensure all measures are taken to provide for any fur-

Fig. 1-3

A panicky diver will usually calm down as soon as he can rest.

- **Communicate**
  Use signals underwater. On the surface, talk to the victim if possible. Shout if necessary. Your voice alone may reassure him, or shock him out of panic. Ask for co-operation. The response will indicate the victim's psychological state.

ther care of the victim. Arrange for victim's equipment and air to be checked.

- **Evaluate**
  Review what happened and why. Learn from the experience!

Summary

General Rescue Principles

- Stop and Think
- Know Your Limits
- Use the Least Hazardous Method
- Enlist Help
- Maintain Visual Contact
- Establish Respiration
- Establish Buoyancy
- Communicate
- Continually Assess the Situation
- Account for the Victim's Buddy
- Follow up
- Evaluate

CHAPTER 2

Preparation for a rescue emergency

Personal skills

The earlier the warning signs, the easier an accident is to avoid. The chain of events leading to disaster may start at any time, frequently before the day of the dive.

Prior to entering the water, correct any deficiencies in your equipment, knowledge, physical fitness, skills, mental alertness and psychological readiness.

In the water, *dive defensively*. This means being fully aware of all that is going on, in order that you can act to correct a problem in its early stages before it becomes serious. Think ahead, dive ahead!

To be a safe diver, base your decisions on all pertinent factors, and admit your limitations. Build self-discipline to control your physical and emotional responses to hazardous situations.

Frequently think through and review the steps you would take to deal with various types of diving emergencies. Such mental exercises will develop an awareness of alternative courses of action and help a rescuer to think clearly during emergencies and to improvise effectively when required. This judgment experience is vital.

Rescue skills should be practiced frequently. A good practice opportunity is the return swim following a dive. One or more rescuers may review rescue breathing with and without lines and floats. Tired from a dive, the simulated victims will welcome a free ride back, and the line handlers will gain valuable

experience. Arrange a signal to distinguish practice from an *actual* rescue.

"Quit while you're ahead." If you terminate your dive before you become unduly tired or cold, you should have adequate energy for coping with the unexpected.

Profit by mistakes. All divers have made some. Share them with your fellow divers. You may save someone's life long before the dive.

Take courses in life saving and lifeguarding. Everybody should have first aid and cardio-pulmonary resuscitation (CPR) training.

Learn how to handle canoes, rowboats, sailboats, motorboats, and paddleboards by attending courses conducted by aquatic agencies and sport organizations. These courses emphasize the use of small craft in rescue work, navigation and safe piloting.

National scuba certifying agencies run rescue and safety seminars, and offer courses in scuba life saving and advanced specialty diving. Take a course in *your* specialty. If you can't take a course, at least read many of the excellent books and pamphlets produced by these agencies. Keep up with your sport!

Good habits can save lives in the water. Practice frequently in order to make your skills automatic. Then, in a rescue your conscious mind will be free for the more demanding aspects.

Your breathing habits can save your life. If you have formed the habit of always regularly venting air as you ascend (slightly, but not enough to negate your buoyancy), you will do so without thinking when you lose your air supply at depth.

The habit of breathing in through your mouth and out through your mouth and nose will prevent coughing or spasms if your mask leaks or is knocked off underwater. Whenever your nose is exposed to water, your inhalations should, from force of habit, automatically switch from nose to mouth.

Many divers assume that just having a buddy along will resolve any possible problem. Unquestionably a buddy can be excellent insurance against disaster—if that person stays with you, watches, and knows what to do.

Pick a responsible buddy who is well versed in life saving. Unless you are willing to bet your life on your buddy's alertness, knowledge and skills, perhaps you should not dive.

In many cases a single buddy is not enough. To handle emergencies, it may be necessary to have two or three rescuers on the dive. For instance, could you, all alone, administer rescue breathing, tow a victim to the boat, get him aboard, start the engine, pull up the anchor, radio for help, and steer the boat while continuing CPR?

Location of emergency equipment

Let's assume you are ashore and have handled the immediate problems, but your fellow diver is still in critical condition and urgently needs medical care. This is no time to search for a *working* phone! That should have been checked on the way to the site. It is also a poor time to start looking up phone numbers. Far better to pull them from your first aid kit, along with the necessary coins. List the emergency telephone numbers on a card and laminate it.

Fig. 2-1

Can you perform a complete rescue alone?

Fig. 2-2

WHAT'S THE COAST GUARD FREQUENCY?

Keep a list of important numbers handy in your first aid kit.

A diver whose buddy obviously has the bends may find himself dealing with a physician who does not understand diving maladies and wants to hospitalize the victim a few days for "observation" instead of rushing him to a recompression or hyperbaric chamber. Get a diving doctor on the phone. Call the Diving Alert Network (DAN) (919) 684-8111, if necessary. A medical professional is likely to listen to a knowledgeable physician who can explain the situation and advise the best treatment.

Communicating a problem

Underwater

Hand signals In an underwater emergency, communication is very important. Thirteen hand signals have been standardized nationally. The first ten are also recognized internationally in over fifty countries affiliated with CMAS (Confederation Mondiale des Activities Subaquatiques), the World Underwater Federation.(See Diagrams 1-13)

Seventeen other signals are also worth learning. (See Diagrams 14-30)

To avoid ambiguities, it is wise to review signals prior to a dive.

A growing trend in diving is learning to sign—the language of the deaf. Underwater communication then presents much fewer problems. An excellent booklet, *Underwater Communication* by Dr. Norris Eastman, Ph.D., (Beverley Publishing Co., Richmond, VA, 1979) describes and illustrates a large number of hand signals for divers adapted from the language of the deaf.

All signals should be delivered in a forceful, exaggerated manner. They should be immediately acknowledged with a nod, or through mimicry, unless the action taken makes it obvious that the message was understood.

One of the most important emergency messages that may need to be given to a diver is for him to exhale. A special hand signal from the language of the deaf is recommended.

National Standard Hand Signals (1 through 13)

1. Stop, hold it, stay there	2. Something is wrong	3. OK? OK.	4. OK? OK. (glove on)

5. Distress, help	6. OK? OK. (on surface at distance)	7. OK? OK. (one hand occupied)	

8. Danger	9. Go up, going up	10. Go down, going down	

11. Low on air	12. Out of air	13. Buddy breathe or share air	

Commonly Used Hand Signals (14 through 30)

14. Come here

15. Me, or watch me

16. Under, over, or around

17. Level off, this depth.
The safe signal used in baseball is also utilized in diving.

18. Go that way

19. Which direction?

20. Ears not clearing

21. I am cold

22. Take it easy, slow down

23. Hold hands

24. Get with your buddy

25. You lead, I'll follow

Commonly Used Hand Signals (Cont.)

26. Yes

27. No

28. Look

29. What time? What depth?

30. I don't understand

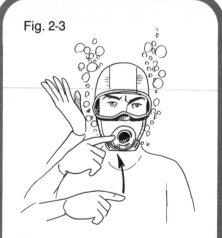

Fig. 2-3

To signal your buddy to exhale use your hand and blow bubbles.

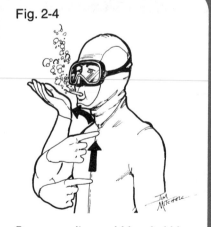

Fig. 2-4

Purse your lips and blow bubbles when you have no regulator inserted.

(drawing from NAUI Proceedings of IQ10)

Slate writing One way to guarantee understanding is to write the message. The "slate" can be a white plastic card or the white back of an instrument console. Use a grease pencil or an ordinary graphite pencil.

Although writing takes more time than talking, it's safer because the regulator is kept in place. Writing also allows two-way "conversations".

Talking Talking underwater is made difficult by the inadequate transmission of sound and the noise of the bubbles as air escapes from the mouth. While these problems can be partially overcome by talking into a glove, or using gadgets, these are not likely to be useful in an emergency. If the listener is not expecting a message, it may be missed entirely. Divers should be breathing in or out at all times. Stopping to listen while inadvertently drifting upward can be dangerous. In

large area. A small air-horn can be sealed in a plastic zip-lock bag and operated underwater. Starting and "revving up" the boat engines (but not the propeller) repeatedly can be used as a recall signal.

Light signals Other ways to attract attention underwater are banging on a tank, or using lights, including strobe flashers or luminous chemical wands.

Obtaining help on the surface

Radio and visual signals Boats in trouble employ many signaling methods. The ideal is to call for help over the radio. Signal flares may be used by distressed boats as well as by distressed divers. Other emergency signals for boats include the Morse code S.O.S. (three dots, three dashes, three dots, given by light or sound), clothing fastened to a pole like a

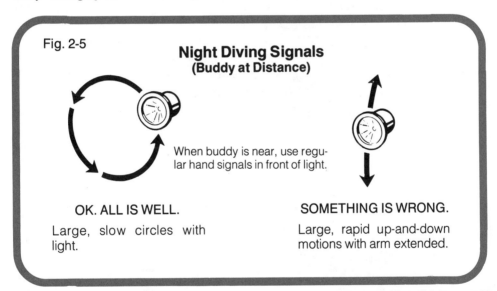

Fig. 2-5

Night Diving Signals
(Buddy at Distance)

When buddy is near, use regular hand signals in front of light.

OK. ALL IS WELL.

Large, slow circles with light.

SOMETHING IS WRONG.

Large, rapid up-and-down motions with arm extended.

an emergency, however, *yell* through your regulator. If your buddy is between breaths, you may attract his attention.

Sound signals Recalling divers from the depths is much more difficult. Sounds that carry easily in the air don't penetrate water well. Underwater speakers are fine in a pool, but their range in open water is limited. One system is to hammer on an underwater metal ladder. The range is short. A loud siren can usually be heart underwater over a fairly

flag, flag flown upside down, smoke, flames (oily rags burning in a metal pail or pan), or continued intermittent blasts on an air horn.

Attention can be attracted with a mirror which reflects sunlight. Mirror signals aimed at the horizon have been seen by pilots over 32 kilometers (20 miles) away. A mirror may not be necessary. Clear glass also reflects light. Use a windshield, a mask, or the face of an instrument dial.

You can signal without any equipment by waving your outstretched arms. If you hold a bright cloth in each hand you will be more visible. If you can get close enough, hail another boat. They may be able to radio for help. Ask them to stay with you. Maritime law requires assistance to vessels in distress.

Every diver should have a whistle. It is frequently fastened to the BC inflator hose. Five or more short blasts is an international distress signal.

Flags We all recognize the red and diagonal white "divers down" flag. Less familiar is the internationally-recognized code-flag "A," which also means, "Divers below, stay clear at slow speed."

Another international code-flag you may not know is "P," which means, "Return to ship." It can be used to recall swimmers, snorkelers or divers on the surface. First, of course, you'll have to get their attention. Use a siren, whistle, bell, air horn, or public address system.

Other equipment Aboard a boat, all divers should know the location and operation of personal flotation devices (PFDs), fire extinguishers, first aid kits, oxygen tanks, resuscitators, and other emergency equipment. Boat dives are ideal for safety and emergency procedure briefings; you have a captive audience.

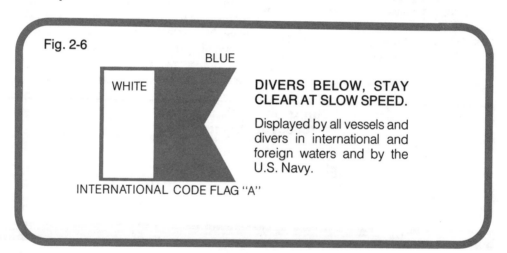

Fig. 2-6

BLUE

WHITE

DIVERS BELOW, STAY CLEAR AT SLOW SPEED.

Displayed by all vessels and divers in international and foreign waters and by the U.S. Navy.

INTERNATIONAL CODE FLAG "A"

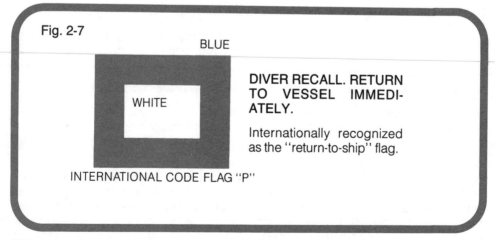

Fig. 2-7

BLUE

WHITE

DIVER RECALL. RETURN TO VESSEL IMMEDIATELY.

Internationally recognized as the "return-to-ship" flag.

INTERNATIONAL CODE FLAG "P"

All three above drawings reproduced with permission from PADI Standard Diving Signals, Consumer Information Bulletin #102.

One or more standby divers should be equipped and ready to go into the water. Some standby divers prefer not to wear tanks. Tanks slow progress in the water, and most rescues are made on the surface. However, a full tank with an attached regulator and backpack should be ready for use at a moment's notice.

Non-divers on the boat can serve as bubble watchers. They can record entry and exit times for each buddy pair.

Let someone know where you are going, including possible alternative destinations, your expected time of return, and what steps should be taken if return is delayed beyond an agreed-upon interval. Potential rescuers must know where and when to start looking.

Always call the roll before leaving the dive site. Divers have been left behind!

Fig. 2-8

Summary

Be prepared for a rescue emergency

      Take training courses in life saving
      Dive defensively
      Learn from your mistakes...and those of others
      Practice thinking through potential problems
      Know location of emergency equipment on dive boat
      Tell someone on shore your dive plan

Communicating your problem in emergencies

      Practice standard hand signals
      Write, talk, sound or flash an emergency underwater
      At the surface, radio or visually signal by flares or flags

CHAPTER 3

The diver under stress

Diving accidents do not just happen. There are a series of early warning signs. Frequently small problems build one upon the other. The early detection of these stresses allows intervention before a life-threatening situation develops. Many early warning signs can be recognized long before the dive—inadequate gear, neglect of equipment maintenance, poor physical condition, incomplete training or planning, indulgence in alcohol or drugs.

Attitude check

A diver who is not mentally ready for the water may betray anxiety in a number of ways: an increase in voice pitch, incessant chatter, gallows humour, or shrill nervous laughter.

The reluctant diver may hesitate during dive preparations, making false starts or stepping back frequently to get equipment. He may simply withdraw and allow himself to be left out when buddy pairs are assigned or ask to be the last diver.

A diver may invent a multitude of artificial reasons for not going into the water, but will seldom admit fear. If, after a number of excuses are resolved, the hesitant diver still conjures up an additional excuse, it should be apparent that he just does not want to dive on that day. Allow him to save face and accept his last excuse.

No one should ever humiliate, or coax into the water, a person who claims he should not dive because of a cold or respiratory congestion. Any slight congestion in one of the lung's small branching airways could block the flow of escaping air, causing a rupture. Such congestion can remain for weeks following a severe infection. Even if you feel the individual is malingering, allow him to be excused. This excuse has probably prevented accidents caused by a diver over-extending himself.

Discourage consumption of alcohol, carbonated drinks, gaseous foods, etc., before or after a dive. Alcohol gives a false feeling of warmth while increasing the possibility of body core chilling. More seriously, alcohol depresses the mental and physical state of the consumer. Blood alcohol levels of .05% to .15% (equivalent to only a few drinks) may make a diver foolish and careless in the water. At a level of .3% you won't care enough to save yourself. Alcohol after a dive can precipitate the bends. Carbonated beverages are well known to do so.

Equipment check

Fellow divers should know the type, color and individual characteristics of the gear each is wearing. The only otherwise recognizable feature of a fully suited diver is his face. Even that depends on a full front view and sufficient light, which is frequently lacking underwater. If you have memorized the gear a given diver is wearing, you will always be able to identify him. One caution: Don't depend too much on colors—they change underwater.

Many accidents result from divers allowing each other to go into the water ill-equipped. Be certain that each item of gear is adequate for the presumed conditions, that it is in working order, and that it is positioned to serve its purpose while not interfering with the operation of another piece.

Equipment checklist

____ Diving suit to fit the conditions. Zippers and velcro fasteners closed. Crotch strap secured.

____ Hood, gloves, and boots in place where necessary.

____ Snorkel in place.

____ Mask de-fogged and in place. Strap locked securely after adjustment.

____ Buoyancy compensator in place with straps secure. Check for proper tightness of straps, and operation of over-pressure valve during an oral test inflation. Inflator mechanism, if any, connected and operable. CO_2 cartridge intact and firing mechanism operable. Whistle attached.

____ Tank secure in backpack at right height.

____ Regulator over right shoulder and operable.

____ Air *fully* turned on with adequate pressure. Do not turn an open valve back partially. It is too easy to confuse this procedure with its opposite (partially turning on a closed valve). Such a slightly open valve will deliver adequate air flow in shallow water, but will appear to shut off at depth.

____ Spring actuated reserve, if any, in proper position.

____ Tank straps secure and not covering hoses or buoyancy compensator.

____ Adequate weights in belt (or weight system), positioned to avoid shifting.

____ Quick release buckle on belt with belt positioned free to drop. Or weight release system operable.

____ Weight belt not covering hoses.

____ Working watch or bottom timer and depth gauge in place.

____ Knife sharp, secure, and properly positioned for conditions.

____ Fins on with straps locked in place.

Equipment insufficient for the conditions can be dangerous, but so can too much equipment. Concentrate on one underwater activity at a time.

During the pre-dive check, both the diver and his buddy should go over the operation of their own and each other's gear. Note the colors of belts, the positions of buckles, and the distinctive characteristics of buoyancy compensator inflator mechanisms. Both should be certain they can operate their own *and* each other's gear with eyes shut in simulation or poor underwater visibility.

Discuss with your fellow divers the peculiarities of the dive site: depth of the water, height of the waves, strength of the current, type of bottom. Depending on the conditions, set a maximum depth, a maximum bottom time, and a minimum amount of air to save for the surface. Discuss any existing hazards or possibilities for trouble. Do not hesitate to cancel a dive if problems cannot be easily overcome.

Signs of trouble once submerged

By its nature, diving does not allow easy detection of danger signals. Facial expressions and skin color changes are masked, verbal communication is practically non-existent, visibility is typically curtailed, and long distances may separate buddies from each other and from the boat or shore.

the subtle behaviors you may observe:

- *Grasping* an object above the surface tightly with both hands and trying to climb higher may signal an effort to escape from the water.
- *Changing* speed or direction abruptly could be a sign of trouble. Lagging behind or swimming away from a group can cause obvious problems.

To recognize a problem you must be attentive.

Because diving problems are difficult to anticipate, scuba enthusiasts have to be remarkably attentive. To keep a life-threatening problem from escalating, you must first recognize that it exists. You must sense that something unusual is happening—something not quite right.

You may hear something (if you are listening). A whistle, a call for help, or a loud banging are obvious attention getters. But would you notice an increase in your buddy's breathing rate?

You may see something (if you are watching). A diver on the surface, mask thrown off, clawing the air, treading water furiously, eyes like saucers, will quickly draw your attention. But would you suspect that a diver motionless on the bottom—even though regularly cycling bubbles—might be unconscious?

The following are only a sample of some of

- *Diving alone* almost always indicates trouble for a diver or his buddy.
- *Inattention* to a challenging task such as adjusting gear while in the surf zone.
- *Surface orientation* by an underwater diver may indicate that he is uncomfortable and would rather be where there is plenty of air.
- *Ascents at the wrong time or place* can indicate trouble—too late following a planned no-decompression dive, too early from a staged decompression stop, down current from a boat, amid a kelp bed, or into an active boat channel.
- *Leaving the water* through a rip current or heavy surf can lead to trouble. A person tumbling in the surf already needs help. Fatigue at the end of a dive may make even the most simple exit difficult or dangerous, especially getting into a boat when waves are high.

Do not linger in the surf zone.

- *Breath hold divers* should be watched. Anyone who: hyperventilates more than a few breaths; over extends his time, distance or depth; or who exerts himself underwater, is likely to blackout.
- *Bubbles* may be a clue to diver troubles. Continuous bubbles rather than intermittent groups could indicate a free-flowing regulator. If bubbles cease, the diver is not breathing. Immediate action is necessary.
- *A distress or help signal* obviously means trouble. A raised arm, waving and slapping the surface, is the accepted signal for distress. However, you may see only a momentary raising of an arm followed by disappearance under the weight of that arm, or a frantic struggle to stay afloat.

A diver signalling for help may disappear under the weight of his arm.

Panic

There is one underlying factor in almost all diving emergencies—stress. Stress may be the result of a real problem, such as an injury from a dive boat propeller, or it may be a completely imaginary problem conjured up by a fearful diver.

as if it had to operate without a functioning brain. Movements are jerky, ineffective and uncoordinated. Perceptual narrowing occurs. Pointless actions may be repeated over and over. Conversely, in passive panic the diver is literally frozen with fear. This person appears to be in a state of shock and does nothing.

Fig. 3-4

Stress can overstimulate the imagination.

A certain amount of stress will exist in all but the most peaceful dives, and it need not cause any problems. Some kinds of stress—a shark close enough for a good photograph—may even add to your pleasure. However, one intensely stressful episode, a continually annoying stress, or several small stresses, perhaps with mistakes building one upon the other, can quickly turn into panic. This is blind unreasoning action based upon fear. *Panic is the diver's worst enemy.*

Panic is a primitive response. The gray matter of the brain relinquishes control, and the lower nervous centers take over. Primitive movements, including fight, flight or withdrawal, dominate. For divers, panic is an overwhelming sense of not being in control of one's environment, equipment, or self. In active panic, the eyes open wide and shift about, breathing rate increases, the heart beats faster and blood is shunted from the gut to the limbs. The diver's body is responding

Case studies of scuba accidents indicate that panic, resulting in inappropriate actions, has killed many divers even though the initial stress was an extremely minor, non-threatening event.

A diver's mask floods. He inhales a few drops of water through his nose, sputters, and streaks for the surface holding his breath. Result—a ruptured lung.

Another diver, out of air, negatively buoyant, and completely fatigued by a long post-dive swim, gets a mouth full of water. Paralyzed with fear, the diver gives up and silently sinks to the bottom—weight belt in place, and BC not inflated.

The actively panicked diver unthinkingly takes the wrong action. The passively panicked diver takes no action at all.

Since stress is the cause of panic, we should do everything we can to recognize and eliminate stress-producing situations. If stress is allowed to build without intervention, panic will likely follow.

Signs of panic Most of us know the classic signs of an actively panicked diver. He may snatch and keep your regulator, or frantically dash for the surface, clawing and kicking, probably holding his breath and forgetting to drop his weight belt. Upon reaching the surface, he will probably throw off his mask, spit out his regulator, lift his chin high, cough, and gasp for air. He will be vertical in the water, finning hard, clawing to stay afloat even

or assume a fetal position and do nothing to help himself. Underwater, he may even let the regulator slip from his mouth and not attempt to replace it. If he is not moving, even if he is cycling bubbles regularly, he may be unconscious.

On the surface, if not buoyant, the passively panicked diver will sink with no commotion. If buoyant, he may be face down, possibly not breathing through a snorkel or regulator. He will probably make no effort to swim to safety. Whether his face is up or down, always check a motionless diver for consciousness and breathing.

Fig. 3-5

IS HE CONSCIOUS?

A motionless diver may be unconscious.

though one or both arms may be loaded with goodies he is trying to retain.

His eyes will be as wide as saucers. There may be wild, uncoordinated flailing of arms and legs, even if the victim is fully buoyant. If not coughing or sputtering, he will probably be breathing fast, either hyperventilating or panting with shallow breaths. He may be screaming for help but deaf to those who are telling him how to help himself.

Passive panic is less easily recognized. The diver may show no obvious distress. Accordingly, he is not as likely to be rescued. He will probably be motionless. He may hang limply

Self-rescue If *you* begin to feel stress building, or are suddenly confronted with what seems like an insoluble problem, STOP AND THINK. By doing nothing for a moment, you give your brain time to analyze the situation and to consider solutions. Think positively. If you let yourself believe you are going to die, you might do just that—before your time. Concentrate instead on the problem. Determine the cause. Weigh alternative solutions. Pick the best one and try it. If your first solution doesn't work, keep trying others until one does. Don't give up. You are capable of much more effort than you realize.

Rescue of others When attempting to assist an actively panicked diver, be extremely cautious. Do not allow yourself to be snared by his frenzy. If you have to struggle with him, the stress will seriously reduce your effectiveness and may even cause *you* to panic.

You can handle the passively panicked diver almost as if he were unconscious. But be wary. He may suddenly become active.

The complete rescue of both types is discussed fully in Chapter 10.

Summary

Before submerging ask some critical questions

Divers owe it to themselves and each other to insist on rigorous pre-dive checkouts of both equipment and physical and emotional readiness. A stressed diver is not a safe diver. Be alert for the signs of a diver under physical or emotional stress.

Learn the signs of impending trouble

Recognition is the crucial element in preventing the escalation of minor trouble into life-threatening dimensions. A knowledge of and alertness for signs of impending trouble should include an awareness of certain diver behaviors which can signal accident potential.

Panic

Inability to control or modify the stress-inducing variables can lead to panic. Panic results in active or passive behavior in a diver. Be extremely cautious in rescues involving panicked victims.

CHAPTER 4

Cold water, currents, dams and weeds or kelp

This Chapter reviews the environmental hazards of cold water, currents, lowhead dams and weeds, kelp or other entanglements. Every diver should be made aware of these hazards prior to the dive. A review of self-rescue and how to rescue others should be completed prior to the dive.

Cold water

Hypothermia means, "not enough heat". Physiologically, it describes a subnormal, internal (body core) temperature. For divers, prolonged immersion in cold water is the usual cause. Even relatively warm water will rapidly carry away body heat.

Critical temperatures

In water less than 24°C (75°F), clad only in a swim suit, exercise will not warm you, in fact the cold water carries away body heat. The colder the water and the more you move about, the greater the heat loss.

Below 10°C (50°F) the blood vessels in the skin (which constricted on first entering the water and thereby conserved your heat) open up to allow the blood into your chilled skin layers, a process called "cold vasodilation". The surrounding cold water quickly carries this heat away and the body's core temperature drops precipitously.

Risk of hypothermia is influenced by many factors in addition to exercise and water temperature. These include: natural body insulation (fat tends to keep you warm), body build (short and stocky fares better than tall and thin), body size (large people stay warm longer than children), environment (Eskimos versus tropical islanders), and general physical condition (the efficiency of the body's temperature regulating mechanisms).

Of all the factors influencing core temperature, external insulation is the most important. Even wet clothes can reduce body cooling over 50% and generally prevent the cold vasodilation that would otherwise occur in water below 10°C. Of course, wet suits and inflatable dry suits keep the wearer much warmer for much longer. But even with such extra protection, there is the problem of failing to rewarm adequately following a core-chilling first dive. Get your core temperature back to normal. One way is to exercise until you perspire.

Cold shock

Sudden dousing in icy water without adequate protection causes breathing problems—a feeling of not being able to get enough air, even though hyperventilating uncontrollably. An inhalation at the wrong time can result in a coughing fit, a laryngeal spasm, or water in the lungs.

The shock of intense cold on the skin may also cause serious irregularities in the heart's electrical activity. The combination of all these problems may cause the heart to beat inadequately or to stop beating altogether.

When diving in icy water, be well-covered with thick, close-fitting neoprene including your hands, head, feet and neck, and have that easy-breathing regulator in your mouth, so if you gasp and breathe heavily from the shock you can do it underwater.

Hypothermia

The earliest sign of profound hypothermia is uncontrollable shivering. Other symptoms include: slowed reaction time, loss of small muscle dexterity, numbness, speech impairment (victim may appear to be drunk or drugged), poor reasoning ability, loss of memory, decreased will to struggle, and eventual unconsciousness. The skin will be cold to touch and it will usually be gray, or blue. However, it may be red if the outermost blood vessels have opened up from cold vasodilation.

Self-rescue

If shivering uncontrollably, abort the dive and get out of the water. If unable to do so, and you are having trouble coping, remember that larger muscles still operate long after smaller muscles have become useless. If your fingers are too numb, you may be able to release a weight belt with the side of your hand. Or, two hands together might grasp an inflator that one hand could not. Be prepared for muscle cramps which are common when muscles are cold and tired. If you feel a cramp coming on, stretch the muscle until you feel relief. Then change your kick to use a different set of muscles. You will need buoyancy if incapacitated. Do not hesitate to call for help, if necessary. Perhaps someone can throw you a line-and-float for a quick ride back. But with numb hands you may not be able to hold on. Wrap the line around your arm or body.

Should you find yourself in cold water, inadequately insulated, and without any possibility of immediate rescue, conserve body heat by making yourself as buoyant as possible and remain still. The largest areas of heat loss are the head and neck, groin, the sides of the chest. Curl up into a fetal position—upper arms tight against the sides of the chest, forearms over the front, thighs tucked to protect the groin, head out of the water—in order to conserve heat in these areas. This is called the *Heat Escape Lessening Posture—HELP*. Even clad in a wet suit, prolonged exposure

Fig. 4-1

Conserve heat using the HELP.

will eventually chill the body. A buoyancy compensator should keep your head out of the water. Your mask will keep waves and spray from your eyes and nose. Your snorkel will allow you to breathe above any chop. If you stay still and maintain the HELP posture you won't need much air. If you have no flotation, tread water, especially if you have fins. Drownproofing (survival floating with your face in the water) is not recommended in water 15°C (60°F) or colder because of excessive heat loss from the head and neck.

When you see it in your buddy, get him out of the water. Just making him surface can be a big help. The water is usually warmer on top, and his wet suit will expand and give him better insulation.

If you suspect critical hypothermia, ask your buddy. If he admits distress, or is clearly weak, tow him to safety. Handle him gently and do not let him exercise. But *you* may be in the first stages of hypothermia yourself. Simple tasks, easily accomplished in warmer

Fig. 4-2

Groups can conserve heat in the huddle position.

If your buddy is not panicky, and both of you have adequate buoyancy, try the "huddle"— bodies pressed close together to conserve warmth in the trunk area. This technique is recommended for two to four persons. Face inward and grasp each other closely across the shoulders with legs wrapped together. Huddling this way, faced in different directions and looking over each other's shoulders, you are in a good position to spot anyone who might come looking for you.

Rescue of others

In the water, many of the early signs of hypothermia will not be obvious. Continuous shivering is still the principal danger signal.

water, may now be difficult or impossible. You may think you can handle the victim, but the cold may hinder your judgment. Your extra effort, and the warmth you lose from the heavier breathing involved, may drain your heat reserves.

Remember, if your fingers are too numb, use your hands and arms to manipulate victim or gear. Avoid kicking too hard thereby avoiding muscle cramps.

The physical activity in order to rescue someone in cold water means heat loss and further risk of hypothermia to you. If any additional help is available, use it. Air mattresses, paddleboards and boats could all be useful for getting a victim out of the cold water and into the warming sunlight.

Rewarming methods

Get the victim warm quickly but with precautions. If possible, warm the trunk first, without warming the arms and legs. Sudden heat to the extremities will dilate the small blood vessels feeding the skin. This takes the relatively warm core-temperature blood away from the core of the body and sends it to the extremities. Cold, stagnant blood is then returned to the heart and may further depress core temperature (afterdrop).

A warm drink (non-alcoholic) sweetened with sugar should be given to a conscious victim. An unconscious person should never be given anything to drink.

Recent studies indicate that warm moist air aids in raising the core temperature. In hospitals, hypothermic victims are given pure oxygen heated to 50°C (122°F). At a dive site, a rescuer can breathe oxygen and then blow it, warmed and moistened by his lungs, into the victim. This can be accomplished more easily if the O_2 tube is disconnected from the mask and placed in the corner of the rescuer's mouth. You can pass the O_2 tube through a thermos of hot coffee, or a bucket of hot water to warm it even more.

Meanwhile, a tub of hot water might be prepared for immersing the victim's body. It should be maintained at about 40-42°C (104-108°F). If you have no thermometer, test the water with your arm. It should be almost as hot as you can stand. Use this immersion method only for a conscious victim.

No tub? How about an inflated life raft, a fish locker, or beer cooler? It need not hold the entire body. The arms and legs should be left out to avoid afterdrop but keep them low and uncovered if possible to avoid venous return of chilled blood to the heart. Wet suit pants might be rolled down to the hips. Towels can be wrapped around the head and neck and *kept* soaked with hot water.

If you have no tub, blankets alone will be of limited value. A source of heat is needed. Apply hot water bottles, heating pads, chemical hot packs, or other warm objects to the areas where heat conduction is greatest: neck, arm-

Fig. 4-3

You can obtain hot water from the exhaust of a marine engine.

pits, sides of the chest, head, and groin. Ensure the warm objects are wrapped in cloth or wet suits to avoid burning the victim's skin. Key heat loss areas are also sensitive to burns and scalds. Any heat applied should be maintained. Temporary heating will cause vasodilation and afterdrop.

If no other source of heat is available, the victim can be warmed by placing him, stripped

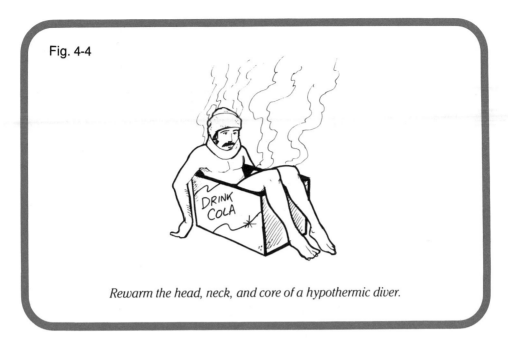

Fig. 4-4

Rewarm the head, neck, and core of a hypothermic diver.

of clothes, in a blanket or sleeping bag with one or two other persons, also stripped.

Shivering is a reliable sign that neither respiratory nor cardiac arrest has occurred.

A deeply hypothermic victim might easily be assumed to be dead. The victim is cold, cyanotic, completely unresponsive with pupils fixed and dilated, and no apparent breathing or heart beat—even when checked by a physician with a stethoscope. However he may be breathing imperceptibly, and his heart occasionally beating feebly, just enough to keep him alive.

In caring for the deeply hypothermic victim on a boat or shore, do not accept a pronouncement of death even by a physician. The victim must be rewarmed, preferably in a hospital, before this vital decision can be made.

Should you start cardiopulmonary resuscitation (CPR) if you are not certain the heart has stopped? A chilled heart, although beating, is extremely sensitive. The pumping action of chest compressions or any other rough handling of this victim may cause ventricular fibrillation, a disorganized quivering of the heart muscles which do not pump the required amount of blood.

However, if the victim's heart is not beating and you do not start CPR, he may die. If no beat can be detected, you have no choice. CPR must be started. If, in doing so, you precipitate fibrillation you won't know it and you wouldn't be able to stop it if you did. But your compressions will be circulating blood. Obviously, CPR will have to be continued, without interruption, until the victim is turned over to a medical facility. There, the victim must be carefully monitored and properly rewarmed before the heart can be stimulated, either by electro-shock paddles or by drug injection, in order to stop the fibrillation and restore normal heart rhythm.

Currents

Ocean and river currents

Currents may be moving so slowly that a diver hardly notices. Or, they may be so swift that they make diving extremely difficult or impossible. Too often divers completely exhaust themselves by attempting to swim against a strong current.

Diving in strong currents is possible because

the current usually decreases with depth. Use a descending line or the anchor line to get down, and while down, swim as much as possible against the current so you can drift easily back to the boat after surfacing. Underwater, the current may shift, and frequently your interest in a wreck or a reef will head you in another direction. If this happens, be prepared for a long, hard swim back when you surface.

Another way to dive in strong currents is to let yourself go. A boat may follow a group of drift divers by watching their float or their bubbles. Or, with no boat, you may plan to exit at another location.

Self-rescue

If you are swimming toward a boat or shore but making no headway or losing ground you need help. A good answer is a line, float attached, thrown or carried to you. A surfboard, paddleboard, or surf mat is another possibility. If all these devices fail, the boat will have to pick you up. (See "Small Craft Rescues" in Chapter 13.)

The current may carry you away when no one is looking. Use your whistle or yell, wave, and slap the water to attract attention. But do not wear yourself out. Some divers carry signal flares for such contingencies.

If you have saved enough air—you should always save *some* air—consider going back down. Take a bearing on the boat before submerging so you will go straight toward it. The current will not be as strong at the bottom, and you can pull yourself along holding the rocks, coral or wreck. If the bottom is bare, you can dig your knife into the bottom to hold against the current.

If you are out of air but think you can make headway, try to cut your drag. To minimize drag, inflate your BC only as much as your buoyancy requires.

Consider dropping anything you are carrying. The weight and bulk also slows your progress. Ditch your weight belt only if necessary because by doing so your legs may become too buoyant for effective swimming. The more horizontal you are in the water the less drag. Keeping your head in the water will accomplish this also. Use your snorkel or turn over on your back. Look forward occasionally to check your direction.

You may surface so far away you cannot see anything! The waves may be just high enough to block your view of the boat. By

Fig. 4-5

CURRENT →

Rig a water-level line to assist divers.

treading water high while circling, you may be able to spot the boat's mast.

If you cannot make it to the boat, and shore is not too far away, consider swimming to shore. An unknown shore, however, can present problems. You may encounter jagged coral, beds of sea urchins, or simply a long stretch of water too shallow for swimming and a bottom too gooey for walking or even crawling. If you get ashore and are able, try to let those aboard the boat know where you are. They may be frantically searching the bottom for your body!

If no shore is near and it is obvious that you will not get back by swimming or signalling, make yourself buoyant and drift with the current. A good boat captain should know to follow the natural drift to your location. In cold water, conserve heat by assuming the HELP or huddle position while you are awaiting rescue.

Rescue of others

Your buddy has just done a stride entry from the boat. You are surprised at the strength of the current, which carries him back toward the stern. He is in no danger of drifting across the ocean because you have wisely rigged a line with a float 300 feet back. But the boat's gunwale is too high for him to reach, and the smooth hull offers no hand hold. He was planning to swim to the anchor line and wait for you, but now it is obvious he can't get there by swimming. And he is wearing himself out!

The answer is to throw him a line and pull him forward to the bow. While he rests and waits, you can string the rig that should have been there in the first place: a water-level line running from the anchor line to the stern. Then you can enter the water and easily pull yourself forward, hand over hand.

Rip currents

The beach diver should be familiar with rip currents formed when water carried to the beach by waves makes a swift, concentrated return to the sea. Reefs, sandbars, or shore line configurations can direct rip currents, which typically flow at 3-12 mph.

A fully equipped diver can rarely swim faster than 1 mph.

A rip current is detected by the cloudy, discolored water and foam. Where the current is flowing out, the surf will be low or absent. The surest sign is a floating object that moves steadily seaward.

Divers frequently use these currents for a free ride through the surf to the area beyond the surf line where the current disperses. One problem is poor visibility, caused by the current stirring up the bottom.

Unfortunately, divers sometimes make the mistake of trying to reach the shore by swimming *directly* against a rip current. The diver gets nowhere and is soon exhausted.

Self-rescue

If caught in a rip, you may choose to relax and ride it to a point where it dissipates, then circle around and come ashore. Or you may swim diagonally to the current until you are out of it. (See Fig 4-7)

Rescue of others

If you are making a swimming rescue from the shore, the quickest way to reach the victim may be to enter the rip area and let the current take you out. The victim can then be told how to get out of the current. If necessary, the victim may be towed to one side of the current for the trip back.

Longshore currents

Waves striking the shore at a sharp angle generate a longshore current parallel to the beach that will quickly carry you away from your point of entry.

Fig. 4-6

Turbid water flowing seaward through a section where waves are not breaking indicates a rip current.

Self-rescue

The least tiring way to get back to shore is to swim at right angles to the current, straight toward the beach. However, such a current may carry you far down shore into rocks, coral, pilings, cliffs, sea urchins and other hazards. If you want to get straight back to shore at an optimum exit point, swim at an angle *against* the current. The force of the water and the force of your swimming will combine to push you sideways. It *may* take more time and energy than swimming at an angle with or across the current, but it will get you closer to your objective. Use this method to reach a drift line trailing from a dive boat.

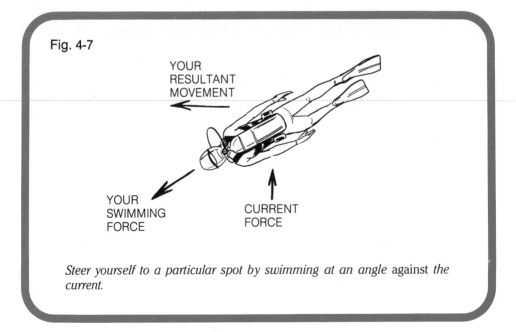

Fig. 4-7

YOUR RESULTANT MOVEMENT

YOUR SWIMMING FORCE

CURRENT FORCE

Steer yourself to a particular spot by swimming at an angle against *the current.*

Fig. 4-8

The re-circulating backwash current below even a small dam can be a treacherous "drowning machine."

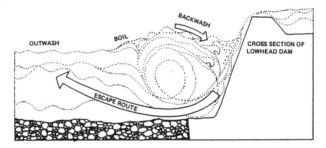

Fig. 4-9

A good swimmer may escape the recirculating current of a lowhead dam by swimming along the bottom beyond the boil—if he is not blocked by bottom debris.

Lowhead dams

Lowhead dams—small dams, with no centralized spillway, that form an artificial, uniform barrier across a stream—are frequently described as drowning machines during high-flow water levels. The big danger is not the generally recognized one of going over the falls, but the unsuspected hydraulic backwash of water below the dam. Even dams no higher than 15 cm (6 in.) can create this treacherous re-circulating action.

If caught in the backwash, you will be carried to the face of the dam where the falling water will force you under, then down-stream along the bottom to the upwelling "boil", where you will be brought to the surface—only to be swept back and battered under the falls again. This cycle continues unless you are caught on debris under the falls.

An added problem is frothy water on the surface that may be so thick that it covers your head. Breathing under it is almost impossible.

Self-rescue

If you keep your teeth clenched, some air may be strained from the froth. If you have scuba air, keep your regulator in your mouth.

If you are a good swimmer you may be able to

Drawings by Louis Trebari. Reproduced from River Rescue *with permission of Ohio Dept. of Natural Resources Instructional Materials Laboratory of the Ohio State Univ.*

control your breathing and survive repeated cycles while you work your way to the side. But you are frequently confronted with a high vertical wall, difficult or impossible to scale. Probably the best way to escape is to deflate the BC, sink, swim downstream close to the bottom and surface beyond the boil. This is more difficult than it seems. When you are exhausted from the battering, your regulator is more easily displaced and your breath-hold time will be minimal. Also, bottom debris may be in the way so that even with scuba you could be snagged.

Rescue of others

Rescuing a victim from this recycling back-wash calls for discretion. The rescuers are likely to be caught in the same trap. When it passes the boil, a boat launched from downstream will probably be drawn into the dam face where it will fill with water, swamp, and capsize. A line from the rescue boat to another boat or to the down-stream shore is necessary to avoid this. Lines with a float attached might be thrown to the victim. However, any attempt to drag him over the boil could put too much strain on the float, or the line. Pulling him back a few feet from the dam face and carefully working him to the

side is recommended. This is best accomplished if one or more lines can be shot or boated across, so rescuers from both sides can control the victim.

Entanglement in weeds, kelp or fishing line

If you are swimming underwater and making no headway, you may be pulling against monofilament or polyester fish line. Because it is almost invisible in the water, divers easily get caught. The object snagged could be a tank valve, a spare second stage regulator, a submersible pressure gauge or console, a snap hook, or the strap buckle of a knife, mask, or fin. Quick twisting and turning often leads to a worse entanglement.

Self-rescue

Backtracking may loosen the line. First, lean into the area, then away from it. If that doesn't work, a sharp knife with a serrated edge will easily cut the line. Be careful with that knife. Divers have been known to cut their own air hoses! And keep a firm grip. If the knife is dropped, you may not be able to retrieve it.

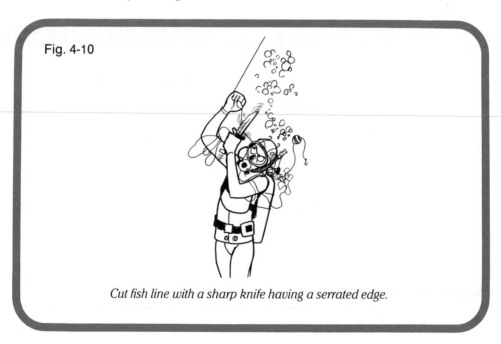

Fig. 4-10

Cut fish line with a sharp knife having a serrated edge.

Fig. 4-11

Paddleboards are excellent for rescues through kelp.

Fishing line cannot normally be broken. But lacking a knife you might try wrapping the line around your forearm so your wet suit provides protection, friction, and purchase, then jerk hard. Alternately, the snagged gear can be removed, untangled, and replaced. Work carefully and methodically to avoid panic. If you remove your tank and still cannot free it, a last option may be considered. Hyperventilate to reduce CO_2 and gain 0_2, leave the tank and make an emergency swimming ascent, venting air as you go. Or, exhale into your BC and re-breathe that air to the surface. (See Breathing From a Buoyancy Compensator in Chapter 7.)

Of course your buddy can help free you. Be still and let him work without your interference.

Kelp and weeds present similar problems to fishing line. Luckily, strands of plant life can be broken by bending and scoring. Or you can pinch and bite the stalks. You may get loose by gently shaking yourself or by dropping down and looking for an open area.

Avoid snags of any type by streamlining your equipment as much as possible—belt snap hooks in the reverse position so they turn inward, knife on inside of leg, buckles under

the sheath, mask and fin straps reversed or taped down, weights unstacked, spare second stage and submersible pressure gauge or console tucked in.

When swimming on the surface through a thick kelp bed, push the kelp down underneath you and crawl forward on your hands and knees instead of ducking beneath it. When swimming underwater through kelp, look forward with your head back to keep the kelp from snagging on your tank valve. Look up to avoid surfacing in thick kelp areas. Pick the open spots. Avoid swimming on your back over kelp. Again, your tank valve may snag. Entanglement is obviously far more dangerous for breath-hold divers. Avoid diving in areas where you might be snagged.

Rescue of others

Paddleboards are an excellent means of transportation for reaching a victim through a weed or kelp bed. With no protrusions on the hull, these glide easily and swiftly over the surface.

To rescue an entangled victim underwater, make certain he has an air supply. Avoid snaring yourself by keeping an arm's length away and remaining perpendicular to him. Signal him to stop and to take it easy so you can free him. Use a scissoring motion with your fingers to let him know what you will be doing behind his back. Then, keeping your distance, trace the contours of the victim's body with one hand and, one at a time, pull his limbs, and then his body, free. When the entangled part is located, cut it loose with knife strokes away from the victim.

Summary

Preparing to meet environmental hazards

Divers should attempt to identify potential environmental hazards which may pose a risk. Having determined the nature of the hazard and the degree of risk involved, the safe diver will avoid the hazard altogether (if possible) or make modifications in his dive plan to reduce the risks.

Cold shock

Sudden immersion in icy cold water may result in cold shock and death to the unprotected diver.

Hypothermia

A reduction in the body's core temperature which must be reversed if a victim is to survive.

Currents

These may sweep you unsuspectingly away. Pay attention to your position, your buddy and your route to safety.

Formed relatively close to the water surface and to shore; one can ride these out until they dissipate, or swim diagonally out of them.

Lowhead dams

Produce a recycling backwash that tends to keep an object trapped in the water's motion.

Entanglement

Entanglement in weeds, kelp or fishing line requires a diver to carefully work away with a sharp knife in order to free himself.

Knowledge, alertness and sensitivity to the signs of potential trouble are the diver's best protection in avoiding environmental traps and dangers.

Rescues involving lost or trapped divers

Lost buddy

How often have you heard the rule, "Never dive alone"? And how often have you seen it violated by some of the most experienced scuba enthusiasts? When two buddies are separated they are both "lost divers." Select a buddy with whom you feel comfortable—and someone who feels comfortable with you. At the water's edge, take the time to ask each other a few pertinent questions. Do you agree on the purpose of the dive? Have you agreed on hand signals? Do you know the placement and operation of each other's gear? Can you recognize your buddy underwater?

Everyone in the diving party should be responsible for only one other diver. If you have to dive in a threesome, No. 1 should be responsible for watching No. 2, who should watch No. 3, who should watch No. 1.

Underwater, try to stay no more than arm's length apart. Buddy lines are helpful in poor visibility. Because you feel your buddy's presence, you do not have to look so often. In super-clear water, divers tend to drift long distances from each other. Simply having your buddy in view is not enough if you cannot get to him in time to help.

By swimming shoulder-to-shoulder you can keep in touch through frequent side-glances and elbow-rubbing. Listen to your buddy's breathing, too. If it fades, you know you are separating. Generally the buddy team should adapt its pace to the slower diver. Divers can easily become separated when the more athletic or rambunctious member of the pair attempts to lead. Moving slowly and deliberately seems to be the best technique in all aspects of scuba. Remember to stay together on the surface too, most accidents occur there.

Self-rescue

Have you agreed on what to do if you are separated? The best procedure is to quickly return to where you last saw your buddy, then pivot 360 degrees looking up and down. If that fails, ascend a few feet, far enough to get above any existing silt. While continuing to turn, look for bubbles and listen for breathing. Allow about thirty seconds for a sign of your buddy, then ascend.

If both of you do the same thing, you will be reunited on the surface, and you can continue the dive. If your buddy does not appear, and you have come straight up, you are now at the starting point for an all-out search. Inflate your BC and fin to get yourself high enough to look for bubbles. Call for help.

Rescue of others

As soon as the missing-diver alarm is sounded, several activities should occur simultaneously. To be certain they do, the divemaster should take charge.

Bearings should be taken on the recently-surfaced buddy, assuming he came straight up from the spot where he last saw the missing diver. Place a marker buoy at the buddy's ascent point. To keep the buoy line taut even in waves, run a line weighted unevenly on both ends through the handle of a plastic gallon jug as shown.

Get the buddy's story. What happened? When? Where? Ask him to furnish a description of the missing diver's distinctive gear, including type, brand, and color. You do not want to mistake a searcher for the missing diver.

Make sure that the missing diver is not on your boat, a neighboring boat, or shore. If you were diving from the shore, see if his gear bag, clothing, and car are still there.

A diver-recall alarm should be sounded. It may bring the missing diver up. If not, the divers answering the alarm can be directed where and how to search.

With all other divers accounted for, the missing diver may be located by spotting his bubbles. Pairs of searchers can follow any unidentified bubbles down to determine their source.

Remind the searching teams not to contact the bottom and stir up silt. If you rise a short distance, your BC can be used to alter your buoyancy. Searchers should make themselves slightly buoyant so their fins aim up instead of down. Even 7m (20 ft) above the bottom, fins aimed down may agitate the silt. Pull yourself along with your hands, or use the shuffle kick in which the fins meet like clapping hands, with the bottom fin remaining stationary to deflect the water's force away from the bottom.

Lights are useful for signalling and for searching in murky water.

As searchers descend, they should scan 360 degrees looking and listening for the missing diver, his bubbles, or disturbances in the silt. Search the bottom thoroughly using appropriate patterns of procedures. Use marker buoys to keep track of areas searched.

Meanwhile, lookouts on the boat or shore, preferably with binoculars, should be watching for any signs of the missing diver. They can see much better from a high vantage point—a cliff, a tree, a top deck, a mast.

Search the horizon, particularly downcurrent. But don't neglect up-current because divers normally swim that way. Assigned lookouts should keep scanning during the search. Polarized glasses help to cut the glare and allow searchers to spot someone more readily on the surface at a distance, or close by under water.

Arrange for relief divers and for extra air. Try

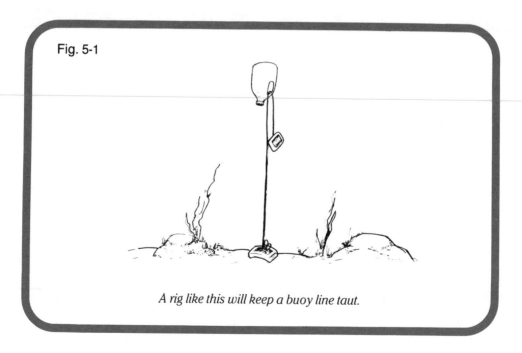

Fig. 5-1

A rig like this will keep a buoy line taut.

getting help from other divers in the area. Some police departments have scuba search teams on call, as well as filled tanks. Ensure that searchers do not forget their decompression times or become victims of exhaustion or hypothermia.

Search actively for at least an hour after the missing diver's air should have run out. If he could have found an additional source of air, for example an air pocket in a wreck, search for a longer period.

After **all possibility** of a rescue has been exhausted, do not endanger anyone's safety in an attempt to recover a dead body. Call for professional help. Recall your searchers.

Search procedures

Formal, organized searches are useful for finding lost objects or dead bodies. They may not be as suitable for locating a missing diver or one in trouble underwater. The advantages of search patterns are obvious. They involve very little duplication of effort, and they leave almost no area unsearched.

But there are disadvantages. Search patterns take time to organize. They may require special equipment. Finally, they do not work well where the bottom is cluttered. Because there is little to see, divers do not normally dive over smooth sandy bottoms; the same visual splendors that attract marine life also attract divers.

Prior planning and preparedness, including practice, can minimize some of these disadvantages. Even in the best of circumstances, it takes time to organize an effective search.

Try the quickest, simplest, and most logical searching methods first.

Random searching

Random, unorganized searching may seem wasteful of time and energy, as it will surely result in some areas being searched more than once while others are missed completely. However, when survival time is running out for a diver underwater, it may be the best method, particularly if the diving area is limited (a small wreck, a kelp bed, a coral outcropping). Saturating the area with undirected divers, pair by pair, as soon as they become available, may locate the victim quickly.

Wrecks and coral reefs, with their blind spots, overhangs, cracks and openings, present special searching problems. The type of opening we are discussing is small. If it contains a diver, he will be immediately revealed when a light is shone in from outside. However, the searcher looking in from "outside" may already be hidden from other searchers by the parts of a scattered wreck or the convolutions of a coral head. Obviously this kind of searching does not therefore lend itself to set patterns. You can start what may appear to be a formal, organized search, but it will not continue for long. The assorted overhangs, cracks, nooks, crannies, canyons, and jagged formations will slow down the searchers and change their directions.

One quasi-formal approach to such small wrecks or reefs involves sending teams of divers in both directions, right and left, around the perimeter. When they meet on the far side, they can start criss-crossing over the top, working their way back to the starting point.

An incapacitated diver will not necessarily be found in the expected area. He may have attempted to reach the surface, blacked out en route, and drifted away from that interesting wreck, reef or kelp bed. Thus, you should know simple searching methods that work well on barren bottoms or in poor visibility.

A diver's sense of direction underwater is very weak unless the bottom topography or the current offers clues. Accordingly, underwater searching over the featureless, currentless bottom requires some method of determining direction. Either a guide line or compass may be needed. Near a wreck, however, a compass will be deflected, so it may be useless.

A few of the more simple search patterns are diagrammed in the next few pages. Depending upon conditions, the less complicated the method, and the faster it can be set up, the better the chances are of locating a victim in time. These procedures or patterns will work well only if practiced with others in advance.

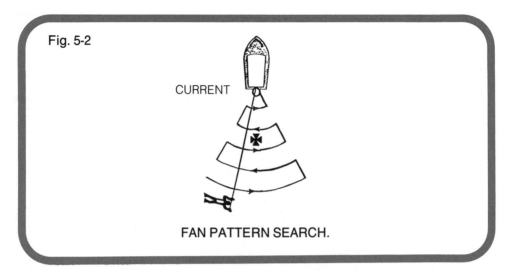

Fig. 5-2

CURRENT

FAN PATTERN SEARCH.

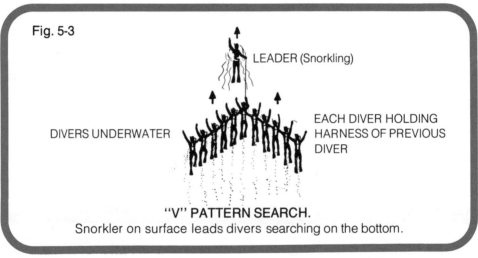

Fig. 5-3

LEADER (Snorkling)

DIVERS UNDERWATER

EACH DIVER HOLDING HARNESS OF PREVIOUS DIVER

"V" PATTERN SEARCH.
Snorkler on surface leads divers searching on the bottom.

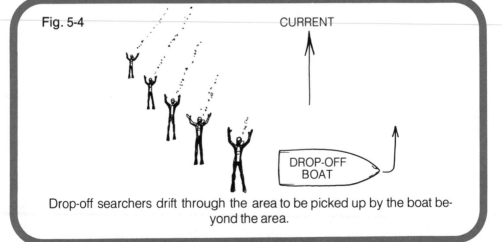

Fig. 5-4

CURRENT

DROP-OFF BOAT

Drop-off searchers drift through the area to be picked up by the boat beyond the area.

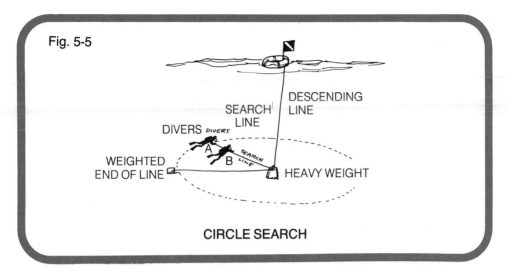

Fig. 5-5

DESCENDING LINE

SEARCH LINE

DIVERS

WEIGHTED END OF LINE

HEAVY WEIGHT

CIRCLE SEARCH

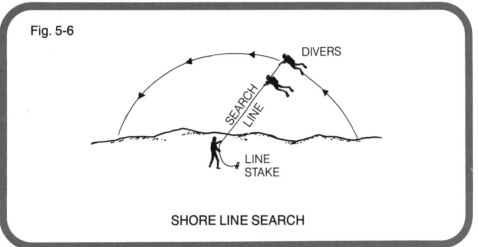

Fig. 5-6

DIVERS

SEARCH LINE

LINE STAKE

SHORE LINE SEARCH

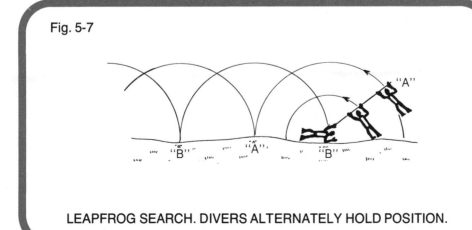

Fig. 5-7

"A"

"B"   "A"   "B"

LEAPFROG SEARCH. DIVERS ALTERNATELY HOLD POSITION.

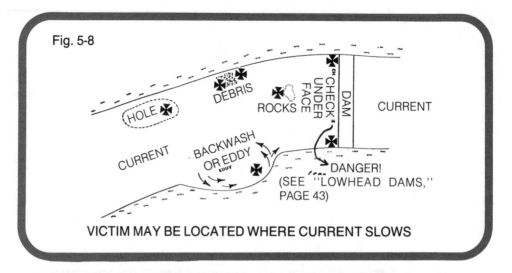

VICTIM MAY BE LOCATED WHERE CURRENT SLOWS

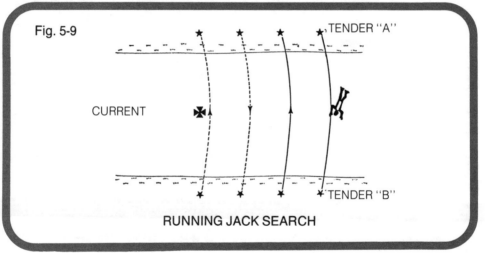

RUNNING JACK SEARCH

Under Cover

Ice diving, cave diving, and penetration wreck diving should not be entered into (literally or figuratively) without adequate instruction. Each requires special equipment, procedures and precautions. This book does not discuss every problem you may encounter in a wreck, in a cave or under ice. The national certifying agencies have courses in these types of diving. Take one before venturing under cover.

Lost under ice

Super-clear water is frequently found under the ice of a lake. However, the location of the entrance hole will not necessarily be obvious from underneath. Diffused by the ice, light will not "stream" as it would through a skylight window. Safety lines are essential. Learning how to rig them and other ice diving safety in a specialty course should precede diving under ice.

Self-rescue

Ice diving instructors suggest some appropriate responses to being lost under ice. Obvi-

Drawings reproduced with permission from Underwater Search and Recovery. *Published by YMCA Center for Underwater Activities. Editor, Stephen J. Hardick*

ously, avoid panic. Stop and think. Look and listen for your buddy, his bubbles, the safety line, and any lights or surface snow path markings that might guide you to the entry hole. If you see none of these things, do not swim around looking for the hole. You may be swimming the wrong way, wasting air. Ascend to the underside of the ice and *stay there*. A dive knife rammed into the ice ceiling can insure that you do not get carried further away from the exit hole by any currents. You can periodically bang on your tank and on the ice and flash your light.

If the ice is less than a few inches thick, it will not support an on-the-ice diving operation. However, if you have wandered under a section of *thin* ice, you *may* be able to penetrate to the surface. Obviously, if you can break the ice from below, it will not be strong enough to support your weight. Call for help, warning your rescuers that the ice is thin. They should approach cautiously with an extension—rope, pole, or branch—spreading out to avoid a dangerous concentration of weight.

You might be able to use your dive knife to chip a small hole, insert a flexible snorkel to breathe surface air. Breathing will not be easy. Extra effort is required to expand your chest against the additional water pressure at that depth. If you succeed, periodic blast clearing of your snorkel may alert topside searchers.

Tests have revealed that, with practice, it takes about ten to fifteen minutes to get through ice about 8-13 cm (3-5 in) thick. The

technique is to hold the knife point against the ice while your other hand hammers with short ramming strokes against the handle. **Caution**: this activity takes a lot of work—and air. If you expect help from above, as you should, it is probably best to relax, conserve your resources, and watch. You do not want to miss seeing the help when it does come.

A lot of people up there can help. A divemaster should be in charge. A tender should be handling your safety line. There should be at least one fully equipped standby safety diver ready to go under at a moment's notice. All of you should have decided as a group how to deal with a lost diver problem.

The safety line tender, when he realizes he is no longer in contact with the diver, should immediately notify the divemaster, telling him the amount of line out and the direction in which it was traveling. If possible, the divemaster should organize two simultaneous searches, one underwater and one on the surface of the ice.

A safety diver should be circling with a drag line to find you. Keep contact with the ice to make sure it does not pass over you, and watch so you will see if it passes under you. Listen, and watch if possible for searchers walking above you. Bump the ice and your tank and flash your light to alert them. If you see the search line secure it and signal to be pulled in. If you happen to follow the line in the wrong direction, you can get air from the search diver.

Rescue of others

A tethered standby diver looking for the missing diver should swim just under the ice heading toward the point where contact was lost. When the line tender notes that there is approximately a third more line than the lost diver had, the tender signals to start a circular search in the direction the diver was last swimming.

Swimming at 1.6 km/hr, (1 mph), it will take a safety diver about 25 minutes to complete a circle search at the end of a 91 m (300 ft.) line. Using a 122 m (400 ft.) line, it will require over 33 minutes.

Keeping the line taut against the under surface of the ice, the standby diver should circle around watching and alert to the feel of the lost diver being snared.

Meanwhile, assuming that the ice is snowless, relatively transparent, and not hopelessly thick or dangerously thin, the topside searchers should be systematically trying to spot (see or hear) the lost diver through the ice. A line of searchers, walking at arm's length apart, can quickly cover a large area. If there is any possibility of thin ice, they should be wearing some type of flotation gear or life jackets or BC. If the diver is found, a hole can be cut for him to breathe and to be helped out. A chainsaw would most likely be the quickest method of reaching the diver. Care should be taken to ensure the trapped diver is not hurt in the rescue attempt. A long-hosed regulator inserted in a small hole will allow breathing while the hole is enlarged through thick ice.

Other rescuers, if available, should cut additional holes beyond the area being covered by the standby divers. Failing entry at the original hole, the standby divers will now have new entry points.

During the search, the victim, the topside rescuers, and the safety divers all risk cold stress and hypothermia. Manual dexterity and judgment will suffer greatly. Safety divers should be rotated if necessary. Provision should be made ahead of time for adequate rewarming of both victim and rescuers. Remember, cold will increase the possibility of bends. Watch dive times carefully.

Malfunction of single hose regulators is very likely, especially when divers are double-breathing with octopus rigs. Extra care to keep moisture from entering breathing gear and to protect it from sub-freezing temperatures will minimize such ice-caused malfunctions. An environmental attachment will keep water from entering the first stage. Pony bottles or complete auxiliary scuba units are better for rescue double-breathing. (The now rare double-hose regulator is much less likely to freeze and free-flow, but it has other drawbacks. Even if a regulator free flows, it can still be safely used if necessary.)

Lost in a cave

Too many divers die inside caves. Without special equipment and training learned in a cave diving course, divers should never enter caves. But divers do go in without adequate preparation, or fail to heed important safety rules, and get lost.

Self-rescue

Experienced cave diving instructors have offered some good advice. Stop and think. Do not swim around aimlessly. This will only stir up silt, increase air consumption and encourage panic. Make yourself buoyant enough to rise above the silty bottom. Turn 360 degrees, looking up and down as well as sideways. Two important clues that can lead you back are the bubbles you have left on the cave ceiling and the silt you have left in the water.[1]

You may see the safety line, your buddy, or the other diver's lights. Consider turning off your light to make others' lights more obvious. It will take a few seconds to become accustomed to the dark. Listen for other divers while you wait. If you hear anyone, or if you see other lights—reflecting off walls, coming around a bend—flash your light up and down and tap on your tank to attract attention. Turn on your strobe light if you have one.

If you fail to see, hear or arouse others, try to find the safety line by calmly moving a few body lengths, first one way and then the other. Better yet, take out the 8-16 m (25-50 ft.) of personal safety line you should be carrying. Anchoring one end, hold the line while you search for the group safety line. It may be at the opposite wall.

[1]Sheck Exley, Basic Cave Diving, *Revised Second Edition, National Speleological Society: Jacksonville, Florida, (0) 1980, p. 36.*

If you find the group safety line, check for small wedge-shaped "Dorff" markers of folded tape which indicate the direction to the nearest exit.

The direction of current flow can also help. Downstream will lead to a spring opening, upstream to a siphon or in-flowing opening. If there is no apparent current, stir up a pinch of silt and watch closely for movement. Even without any detectable flow, the tips of scallops on the cave walls will point in the direction of the prevailing current. A compass can help if you took readings on the way in or studied a map of the cave prior to the dive.

You may find a pocket filled with seemingly breathable air. Assume that it is not safe. It may consist of almost pure nitrogen, the oxygen having been consumed by other divers or through natural iron-oxide formation. If you remove your regulator and breathe the air in the pocket it could smell perfectly fresh. You may not feel any symptoms before you black out a few minutes later! If your tank is empty, however, you should certainly take the chance that the pocket contains oxygen to keep you alive until rescued.

Rescue of others

When they realize someone is missing, the other divers should immediately flash lights around to attract attention. Look and listen for the missing diver. Do not fan up the silt.

Consider having one diver tap on his tank at intervals.

If the lost diver is not located immediately and if there are several divers in the group, one member can be sent back to the surface to alert the standby divers. If you have planned ahead they should be suited up and waiting their turn to dive, preferably equipped with an extra scuba for the lost diver.

Meanwhile the reel man should have tied off the safety line at the point where the diver was missed. One diver should stay at that point. The remainder of the safety line or an extra coil can be used to sweep the perimeter of the cave.

Rescuers should keep track of their time and air consumption, leaving themselves a margin of safety. If the search is unsuccessful, the team should leave the safety line tied off. Its end will show a rescue team where to start their search. Also, the lost diver may find it, as the visibility improves, and save himself.

You cannot handle a victim inside a cave the same way as in open water. If you drop his weight belt or inflate his buoyancy compensator, he may get stuck near the top of the cave, and you'll have to work hard to keep him down.

If you struggle with the victim, you will probably stir up silt, thus reducing your visibility

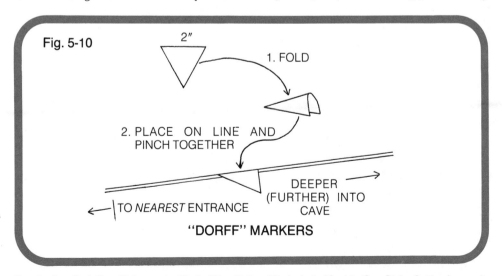

Fig. 5-10

2″

1. FOLD

2. PLACE ON LINE AND PINCH TOGETHER

TO *NEAREST* ENTRANCE

DEEPER (FURTHER) INTO CAVE

"DORFF" MARKERS

Drawing from Basic Cave Diving, *revised 2nd edition, National Speleological Society, Cave Diving Section, by permission of artist and author, Sheck Exley*

and inviting panic. For this reason, *practice* in cave rescue techniques should not be attempted in a cave, but only in open water or a pool. Never stir up silt in a cave deliberately!

If the victim is out of air, time is critical. You will have to share your air, and it will last *less* than half as long due to the increased stress. Octopus rigs, pony bottles, or double tanks yoked together drawing on a common air supply are all obviously better for sharing air than buddy breathing. Whatever the method, continued contact with the safety line is essential. If the out-of-air buddy can be given an extra long regulator hose or detachable pony for breathing, both buddies can go single file through narrow passages. If the airless buddy stays in front of the rescuer, he is not likely to be left behind. Information re the use of a BC as an emergency source of air appears in "Breathing From a Buoyancy Compensator," at the end of Chapter 7.)

If the victim is unconscious, but breathing, hold his regulator in his mouth and tilt his head back to keep his airway open. Watch him as you tow. Be sure he continues breathing.

If he is not breathing, time is of the essence. While there are some possible ways to give air to a non-breathing victim underwater, they are not easily accomplished. If the distance to safety is short it is probably best to get the victim out of the cave and to the surface as soon as possible.

 **All of this still may not help a lost or helpless diver. Prevention is a better answer. Don't go into caves without special training!**

Lost in a wreck

Silt, which can quickly obscure an entranceway has trapped many divers inside wrecks. Penetration wreck diving and subsequent rescue techniques are so similar to cave diving that anyone considering exploring an extensive wreck would be wise to take a cave diving course in addition to a course in wreck diving.

Fig. 5-11

Do not drop a weight belt or pop a CO_2 cartridge in a cave.

There are some differences from cave diving, however. Wrecks are frequently festooned with almost invisible fish lines, hooks and nets. You may get snagged. Carrying two sharp knives (a stiletto as the backup) is recommended. When entering, hatch-ways and bulkhead doors must be secured open to keep them from jamming shut in surge or current. Wrecks are seldom found upright. The walls (bulkheads), floors (decks), and ceilings are usually at odd angles causing disorientation. Rusting, jagged steel can sever lines or tear flesh.

Air pockets inside a steel wreck may be filled with poisonous gases from decomposition or cargo or be depleted of oxygen due to rust formation.

Passageways may be clogged with heavy furniture, partially floating, or precariously suspended, ready to cascade down onto you if disturbed by the buoyancy of your exhausted air. Similarly, rotting wooden timbers or rusting steel walls or ceilings may collapse.

Wrecks do have one distinguishing feature over caves. As man-made objects, their configuration is more regular and familiar. You are less likely to become lost in blind passageways. Other divers are better able to describe the layout before you enter. Sometimes, a blueprint or diagram of a ship is available for prior study. In addition, light is likely to filter into a wreck. If you turn off your light, you may see the exit.

Summary

Lost buddy

Each diver should be responsible for himself and just one other diver. All divers must understand the procedure to be followed if someone goes missing.

Search procedure

While there are a variety of techniques for determining a search procedure, it must be understood that the circumstances of each emergency are unique and will call for quick and informed decision making by the team leader or divemaster. The keys therefore to an efficient search or rescue operation are advance preparation and practice, and good communication.

Trapped diver

Ice, cave and wreck diving can result in unique and difficult rescue operations. Divers engaged in these higher risk activities should take special advanced training that includes the theory and practice of the relevant self-rescue and search techniques and procedures.

CHAPTER 6

Gear problems

Some divers are so dependent upon their equipment that they panic when it is lost or does not operate properly. This chapter outlines methods for coping with such problems.

Your mask drops to the bottom and disappears among the rocks? Without your mask you can't see well enough to find it.

Masks

Self-rescue

If your mask strap breaks and you carry one or two rubber bands on your wrist, you can use these to hold the face plate in an emergency.

Certainly you shouldn't streak for the surface. Instead, if you use your head (literally) and your hands, you can make a "mask" from a bubble of air. The bubble lets you see

Fig. 6-1

Fix a broken mask strap with rubber bands.

clearly enough to retrieve your mask. Look straight down and trap some air in your eye socket(s) with one or both hands pressed tightly against your face. Try the different ways shown in the flounder's eye-view drawings. Use the one that works best for you.

Your wet-suit hood, pulled down but kept tight all around your head will also trap air for making a "bubble mask". Practice these methods in a pool.

If your purge valve leaks and you cannot fix it, remain calm. Just exhale through your nose and keep your face aimed so that the valve opening is at the bottom of your mask. For comfort, block the opening as you inhale. Remain calm and make a normal ascent. You might be able to fix it while on top.

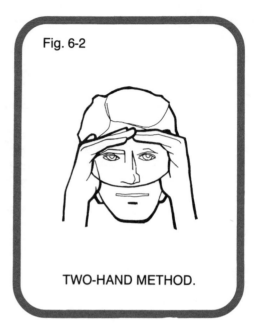

Fig. 6-2

TWO-HAND METHOD.

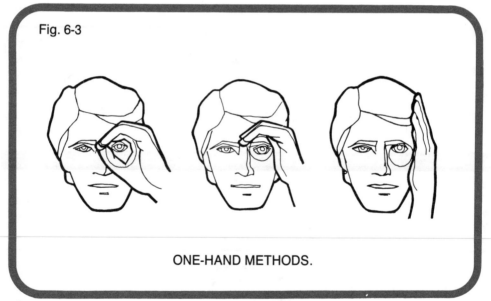

Fig. 6-3

ONE-HAND METHODS.

Lost fins

Self-rescue

A single fin can propel you almost as well as two if you apply the muscle power of both legs. Cross and lock your legs at the ankles and use a dolphin kick. If you have no fins, a scissor kick or breaststroke kick (sometimes called a frog or whip kick) will provide propulsion. Your arms can be used for swimming, or to pull yourself along using any available underwater hand-holds.

Rescue of others

If your buddy loses one or both fins help him find them or show him how to make progress with one or none.

Drawings by Rebecca Salari, reproduced from "See underwater without a mask," Skin Diver, December, 1976.

Regulator Free Flow

You are diving in seventy feet of water. It is a hot day in late March. The water is warm on top, but the temperature at the bottom is 3°C (38°F). Your buddy's breathing, which was slow and easy, now becomes rapid as he struggles, testing his strength by lifting a giant boulder. Suddenly, a constant stream of bubbles pours out of his regulator. It is free-flowing so much air that your buddy has trouble breathing!

If you give him your octopus, your first stage may freeze causing both of your second stages to free flow. Why?

In water 5°C (42°F) or colder, single hose regulators are likely to freeze even though the water is well above freezing temperature.

High-pressure air expands rapidly as it moves from the tank through the first and second stages of the regulator, cooling the metal well below the freezing temperature. Ice crystals begin to form, either on the inside or outside of both stages, interfering with the operation. Freezing can block or restrict air, but the more common hazard is a free-flowing regulator. The volume of air is usually much greater than would result from the purge button being held down constantly. Trying to breathe this air is like trying to drink from a fire hose. And it can empty a tank in only a few minutes! The stream of air may be strong enough to yank the mouthpiece from your grasp, whip it around and make it difficult to retrieve.

Within the critical temperatures below 5°C (42°F), freezing may be precipitated by anything that increases air flow, for example; hyperventilation, simultaneous breathing through an octopus and primary regulator, activating the purge button, or adding tank air to a BC or inflatable suit. Purging a regulator for only five seconds can frequently cause freezing. Moisture in the tank, hoses, or regulator also makes freezing more likely. An environmental attachment will keep water from entering the first stage, reducing the probability of a freeze-up.

Fig. 6-4

You can safely breathe from a free-flowing regulator if you don't close your lips around it, leaving plenty of room for air to escape.

Self-rescue

The high pressure air of a free-flowing regulator could cause a lung rupture. But if you are cautious, you can breathe through one. Grasp the regulator firmly in your hand. Then look down and hold the mouthpiece loosely in your mouth so there is plenty of room for the extra air to escape. You have created a "regulator" so the air you breathe is at ambient pressure. Inhale slowly to avoid strangling on stray droplets. You can now begin a normal ascent to surface.

Rescue of others

If your buddy's regulator free flows and he doesn't know how to use it he may be terrified. How can you rescue him without your own regulator freezing from the increase in air volume? A pony bottle is one good answer.

If you do not have a pony bottle, consider trading regulators. With only one person breathing through your first stage, it is less likely to freeze. Turn off his tank until you need a breath. Then, with his regulator held firmly in your hand, but loosely in your mouth, crack the valve to slowly feed yourself air. The free-flow may cease. If not, keep cracking the valve, turning it off between breaths. You will be able to breathe easily, the tank air will not be escaping too quickly, and, by holding his tank valve, you will be maintaining contact with your buddy.

When both of you are breathing easily, you can ascend together. Your slower breathing and the warmer surface water will tend to thaw the iced-up regulator.

Regulator leaks

A leaking regulator may give you water with each breath. The cause of the leak may be a rupture in the diaphragm of the second stage. If you are not careful, the water will make you sputter, cough or choke.

Self-rescue

If you breathe slowly and cautiously, you can get enough air and no water. It will help if you keep the regulator exhaust valve aimed toward the bottom and exhale frequently to clear the accumulated water. Pushing the purge button may help. You can stop an exhaust valve leak by keeping the exhaust ports down and covering them with your hands when inhaling. Avoid taking quick, strong breaths. If you relax, you will not need such large volumes of air underwater.

Buoyancy compensators (BCs)

Correct buoyancy

Too little buoyancy, too much buoyancy—both can cause problems.

Insufficient buoyancy underwater is indicated when fins angle down and stir up the mud, or when they drag on the bottom.

Too much buoyancy is indicated when the fins are aimed up and beat the water as if the diver were struggling to stay submerged, or when the diver constantly drifts up and away from the bottom.

When your submerged buoyancy compensator has a lot of air around the neck and tends to choke you or keeps your head thrown back, you may be compensating for an overly heavy weight belt. This extra air can be a serious problem when ascending because it will expand and possibly cause an uncontrolled, buoyant ascent. Both weight and air should be reduced before descending.

On the surface, signs of insufficient buoyancy are obvious: head thrown back, fins aimed down, treading water strenuously. The diver may also be clutching a heavy object.

Too much buoyancy on the surface can be a problem. In a full wet suit, or inflatable dry suit, balance may be difficult (if the weight belt is dropped). The excessive buoyancy in the legs may make them pop up. Control may be extremely difficult. A diver may flounder while attempting to keep his legs under him by treading water.

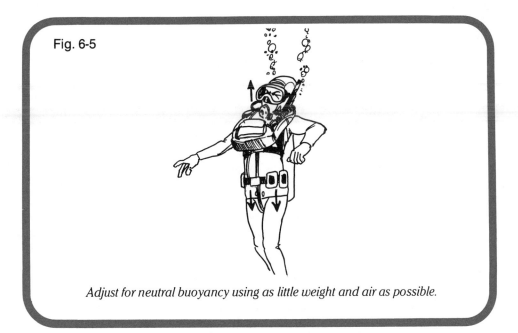

Adjust for neutral buoyancy using as little weight and air as possible.

Self-rescue

A little air in your BC will solve insufficient buoyancy underwater. In an emergency, of course, drop weights.

If too buoyant underwater, release air from the BC. If there is no air in your BC, pick up and carry a rock of the right weight, or hold on to something—coral, kelp, a part of a wreck—and pull yourself along. If you are still too buoyant and struggling to stay down, stop trying. Ascend slowly (flare-out if neces-

If you have no weight belt, your legs may be too buoyant.

sary) and adjust your weight properly on the surface.

Many underwater buoyancy problems can be handled easily without extra air or weights, through controlled breathing. Shallow breaths reduce buoyancy while deeper breaths make the diver more buoyant. These techniques are sometimes easier and safer than using a buoyancy compensator. Extra air and weights increase drag.

The obvious cure for insufficient surface buoyancy is to inflate your BC and drop the weight belt. Buoyancy may also be increased by simply lying on your back with your head in the water.

Inflation and deflation of the BC

"I should have checked that inflator last night!" you say to yourself when nothing happens after pulling the cord. You are diving in the Caribbean without a wet suit, and you have no weight belt to drop.

Self-rescue

If you yell for help into the oral inflator of your BC five times, your help will have already arrived! Your BC will be floating you high in the water.

Remember, you can fill your BC by blowing into it while your head is submerged. However, do not be surprised that your underwater exhalations into your BC do not immediately float you much higher. You are simply transferring the air and buoyancy from your lungs to the BC. But each subsequent surface inhalation gives added buoyancy which will float you higher.

There are four methods of inflating a BC:

1. Orally blowing into the inflator hose.
2. Power inflation, i.e., feeding air through a low pressure hose from the compressed air breathing tank.
3. Puncturing a pressurized cartridge of carbon dioxide (CO_2) gas.
4. Feeding air from a small bottle of compressed air attached directly to the BC.

Most BCs incorporate two or three of these methods, but none use all four. Those BCs using CO_2 cartridges do not use small air bottles and vice versa.

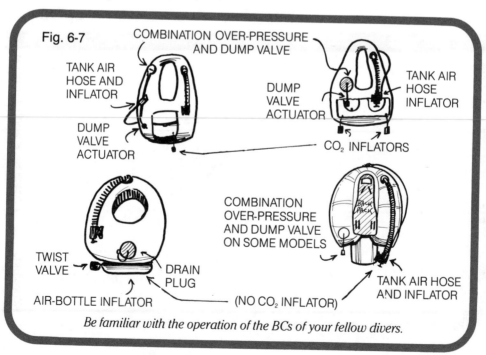

Fig. 6-7

COMBINATION OVER-PRESSURE AND DUMP VALVE

TANK AIR HOSE AND INFLATOR

DUMP VALVE ACTUATOR

DUMP VALVE ACTUATOR

TANK AIR HOSE INFLATOR

CO_2 INFLATORS

TWIST VALVE

DRAIN PLUG

AIR-BOTTLE INFLATOR

COMBINATION OVER-PRESSURE AND DUMP VALVE ON SOME MODELS

BACK PACK

(NO CO_2 INFLATOR)

TANK AIR HOSE AND INFLATOR

Be familiar with the operation of the BCs of your fellow divers.

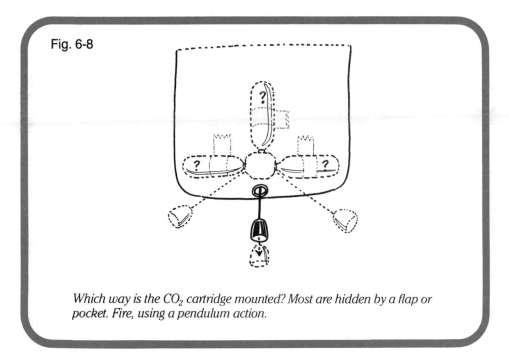

Fig. 6-8

Which way is the CO₂ cartridge mounted? Most are hidden by a flap or pocket. Fire, using a pendulum action.

Some BCs have CO$_2$ cartridges mounted horizontally instead of vertically. Which way is yours? A horizontal position could be troublesome. Most CO$_2$ activators are designed so that a pull on the firing lever in a direction in line with the cartridge, and away from it, will make it fire. If you pull the activator cord of a horizontally mounted cartridge down (as most divers normally would) it may inflate the BC quickly—or the firing pin may move only far enough to barely nick the cartridge. That may make a hole so small it may take minutes to fill the BC.[1] Or, it may not make any hole at all. Obviously, the cartridge must be punctured for the CO$_2$ gas to inflate the BC.

Most CO$_2$ inflator mechanisms are hidden by a flap or pocket with only the activator cord hanging in view. Two problems may result. One is that, even if you do pull the cord correctly away from a horizontally mounted CO$_2$ cartridge, the lever may be prevented from moving in that direction by a grommet.

If your CO$_2$ activator would be so restricted, unthread the cord from the grommet and reattach so it hangs free.

The cartridge may be mounted so that full activation requires a pull toward the left, the right, or straight down. If you do not remember how your cartridge is mounted cover all possibilities: first pull the cord down then swing it back and forth, right and left, like a pendulum.

Unfortunately, the diver who may have to rescue you might not know this.

Inflating a BC with a CO$_2$ cartridge is an all-or-none operation. There is no way to control the amount of buoyancy. If the vest is partially full and has no over-pressure valve, or a malfunctioning one, the vest could rupture from the extra volume of gas and become useless. An over-pressure valve eliminates this problem by venting the excess gas. Remember to check the over-pressure relief valve before the dive by completely filling the BC—then squeezing it. The valve should vent air as you firmly squeeze. If the vest is equipped with a power inflator, it would be easier to check the over-pressure relief valve by activating the power inflation while the vest is completely inflated.

If you *fully* inflate the vest, it can make breathing harder by constricting the throat,

[1]*Michael G. Moore, Presentation of BC Safety Research Findings of the Aqua Amigos Scuba Club, Inc., Cleveland, Ohio, at the YMCA Scuba Convention, Key West, Florida, May, 1979.*

Fig. 6-9

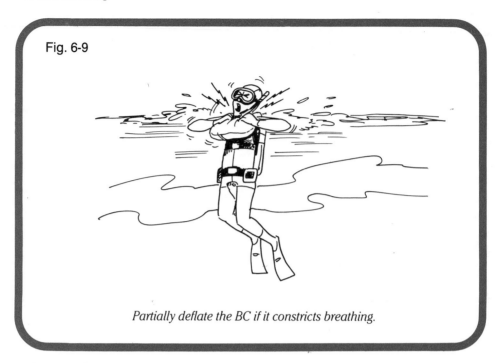

Partially deflate the BC if it constricts breathing.

(especially if there is no crotch strap) or the chest (if the waist straps are poorly adjusted).

You can ease the problem of overinflation by partially deflating the BC. The oral inflator can be used to get rid of excess gas—hold the hose high and open its valve. Some BCs have dump valves to release gas quickly. Others dump air when you simply stretch the hose. The activators of dump valves commonly have lanyards that resemble the CO_2 firing

Fig. 6-10

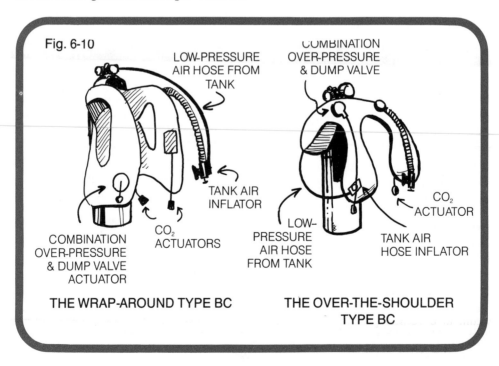

THE WRAP-AROUND TYPE BC

THE OVER-THE-SHOULDER TYPE BC

mechanisms, so be careful not to pull the wrong one. In an attempt to inflate a BC you may dump the air out instead.

Other types of BCs

Backpack mounted buoyancy compensators are generally filled and emptied the same way as those having low-pressure hoses attached to the air tank. Since they are mounted on the diver's back, their buoyancy characteristics are different. An unconscious diver will probably float face down.[1]

Some of the BCs with tank inflator hoses, including the backpack mounted type, will not have CO_2 cartridge inflators. You could be looking for something that is not there! If the tank has been breathed dry, you may not be able to fully inflate this type of BC at depth. (Air may flow into a BC although pressure is insufficient to operate a regulator second stage.) However, there may be enough air for full inflation at the surface due to expansion resulting from the lowered pressure. Otherwise, fill it orally.

Other BCs wrap around or over the shoulders. These types are combined with a backpack and use tank air inflation. Usually they also have CO_2 cartridges. Again, buoyancy characteristics are different.

Tests of one wrap-around type revealed that it must be completely inflated in order to float an unconscious diver's face out of the water. When only partially full, the air shifted to the high side and floated a passive diver on his side—with his face submerged.[1]

Tests of an over-the-shoulder type of BC showed that it would support an unconscious victim in a vertical position. The victim's head would probably flop forward putting his face underwater.[1]

[1] *Ibid.*

Self-rescue

An air leak in your vest? If the vest is leaking from only one side, you may be able to turn that side down toward the bottom so most of the air doesn't escape. Or, remove the vest and put the hole at the lowest point. If it is held at the bottom, near the hole, the air will stay in. You can use the vest as a float. You may be able to control the leak by holding the gathered material in your hand.

Rescue of others

A leak in your buddy's BC will be easier for you to see and control. If he is incapacitated, and the leak is in the collar, you can stop the leak and tow him at the same time. Simply curl the collar up in your hand and use it as a towing handle.

Buoyancy compensator designs are constantly being revised, and many older models remain in use. To be sure you can operate them in an emergency, examine any you are unfamiliar with—on land or in calm water.

Remember, neither power inflators nor CO_2 cartridges will work if they are not properly attached. Check your own and your buddy's.

Inflatable dry suits

Some suits are airtight to eliminate water and keep the diver warm. These can be inflated for buoyancy. Some use only tank air for inflation. Others use only an oral inflator. Some use both. None is equipped with a CO_2 inflator, but a one litre air bottle with hose connections is available for independent suit inflation.

Since the suit itself serves as a flotation device, a diver wearing a dry suit typically does not wear a BC. The bib or horse collar type BC would cover the air intake and exhaust controls of most suits. Look for the inflation control valve at the point where the air hose from the tank connects to either the oral inflator hose or to the suit.

With no inflation capability other than from the main air tank, a diver who has arrived at the surface out of air may be vulnerable. But even though the tank pressure is insufficient to operate his second stage and feed him air to breathe, there still may be enough pressure for some air to flow into the suit through the first stage.

A speedy recovery from a sudden blow-up underwater should be practiced with controlled conditions in a pool. Strong downward kicks combined with either a quick tuck or back arch, depending on the original

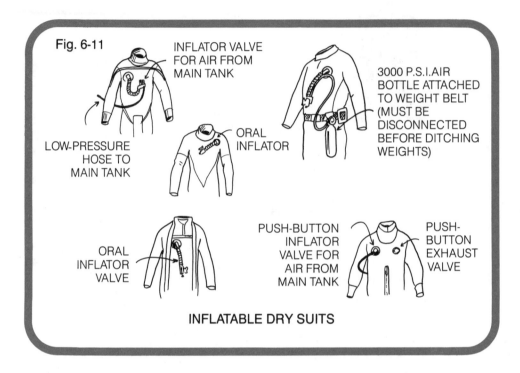

Fig. 6-11

INFLATOR VALVE FOR AIR FROM MAIN TANK

LOW-PRESSURE HOSE TO MAIN TANK

ORAL INFLATOR

3000 P.S.I.AIR BOTTLE ATTACHED TO WEIGHT BELT (MUST BE DISCONNECTED BEFORE DITCHING WEIGHTS)

ORAL INFLATOR VALVE

PUSH-BUTTON INFLATOR VALVE FOR AIR FROM MAIN TANK

PUSH-BUTTON EXHAUST VALVE

INFLATABLE DRY SUITS

Underwater, this may not supply sufficient lift. Dropping the weight belt will add considerable buoyancy and may rotate the diver to a hazardous feet-up position.

Self-rescue

Dry suit divers find that they can usually control excess buoyancy by pulling open a wrist seal or operating the exhaust valve.

position, will right a threatened inversion. Simply raising an arm may then be sufficient to vent air through the cuff.

The buoyancy characteristics of inflatable suits depend upon the style, the amount of air they contain and the fit on the diver. It is possible to inflate some of them so much that the diver has difficulty moving his arms and legs. The enormous buoyancy can make him flounder.

The designs of inflatable suits change constantly, and older models continue to be worn. When you or your fellow divers use an inflatable suit you should know how it performs with and without a belt and with different degrees of inflation. If you learn how these suits react in calm water, you will be confident when assisting yourself or others in time of difficulty.

Weight Systems

Weight belts and tank straps look alike and have similar fastenings. In your pre-dive check with your buddy, you should have noticed the belt color and type of buckle for each. The only way to be certain which is which is to see or feel a weight and follow its belt to the buckle. Most divers wear their weight belts so the buckle can be released by pulling the buckle flange to the wearer's right side. If the belt is fastened with velcro, there will not be a buckle.

Belts may loosen when the wet suit compresses at depth. Gravity may then cause the weight to slip around to the front, carrying the buckle to the back. Minimize this result by using an expanding belt, or simply by positioning the weights toward the front.

Some weight belts lack separate weights and are recognized by their bulk filled with sand or lead shot pellets.

A number of weight systems do not use a belt. In some, weights are stored inside hollow members of the pack frame. Other non-belt systems are attached to the tank. Lead shot, specially shaped weights and even rocks may be used in some systems. Pins, doors and other types of releases are used. Some releases do not work well unless the diver is positioned head-up and roughly perpendicular to the bottom. You should know how to jettison the weights of those with whom you will be diving. DON'T USE WEIGHTS THAT CAN'T BE RELEASED QUICKLY!

A weight belt represents a monetary investment. But there is another reason why commanding a victim to drop the belt may be useless. He may not be *able* to remove it, much less hand it to you while he is using both arms to stay afloat. You may have to remove it for him.

To be sure a belt is completely jettisoned, pull it clear of his body before releasing. If partially loosened, it may hang up behind his back under the tank, or snag on his knife sheath or fins.

Summary

Gear problems are of two types

1. Failure of equipment. This is rare if equipment is well maintained.

2. Diver error in not understanding the limitations or characteristics of the equipment, or the effect of the environment on equipment performance.

Both problems are minimized by adequate training and practice.

Gear problems underwater would be substantially reduced if surface pre-dive checks were sufficiently stringent.

Because gear problems underwater will continue to occur, it is essential that divers understand how to solve, at least, the common problems.

CHAPTER 7

Loss of air supply

"I can't breathe! What's wrong? I had plenty of air for my last breath. Now nothing!"

Given adequate training with equipment available today, this should *never* happen. But it does.

Stop, think, and breathe

The first step for an out-of-air situation is to "stop, think, and breathe". This may seem completely unnecessary, however, this simple check could almost eliminate a tragic phenomenon: the drowned diver who is found wearing a working regulator and tank with plenty of air.

Divers frequently think they are out of air when, in fact, they have simply over-breathed their regulators, usually by strenuous exercise at depth. If it happens, stop all activity, think, ascend slowly and breathe. You will catch your breath.

A similar problem results from fast, shallow breathing in which only the dead air spaces are adequately ventilated. The remedy is the same: Stop, think and breathe more fully.

Sometimes a diver fails to exhale sufficiently between breaths, so that he can't inhale against his own lung pressure. Not knowing the cause of his problem, he assumes his equipment is at fault. If he stops to think and *exhales* as well as inhales, the problem will vanish.

Equipment problems

More than once a diver, forgetting he turned his air on, has unwittingly turned it all the way *off* and back a half turn. The resulting constricted orifice made him believe he was out of air at 1500 psi! Avoid this by habitually turning your air all the way on and not turning it back at all.

When you are panicky, or even under mild stress, you may not remember what gear you are wearing. This is especially likely if it is rented, borrowed, or newly acquired. For example, if you are using a spring-activated reserve "J" valve, you could easily forget you need only pull it down to have enough air for surfacing. Under similar circumstances, you may forget that you have a pony bottle!

Auxiliary air supply

Unquestionably, the best solution to an out-of-air problem is a back-up supply. A pony bottle with a separate regulator attached, or a new type of bailout bottle that has the regulator built into the unit, are becoming recognized as appropriate answers to this situation. But what to do when you simply have no air left from *any* source?

Self-assessment

Consider yourself first. How much breath-hold time do you have? If you ran out of air during a strenuous or stressful activity, you'll have less time. Are you experienced in buddy breathing or emergency swimming ascent? The thoroughness of training and the frequency of practice sessions determine your confidence.

Other divers

Maybe someone has air to share. Is another diver with adequate air close enough to help? Dives should be planned and conducted so this is always the case. Can you get his attention? You'll know his training and emergency experience if you have practiced together. Are you willing to trust this diver with your life?

Water environment

Even if a buddy recognizes your predicament, the water environment may not permit his help. For example, clear water is deceptive. Seeing your buddy is of no use if he is too far away. Buddies should remain close enough to render immediate assistance. Conversely, buddy breathing on a silty bottom could be treacherous. If the water is cold, numb or gloved fingers will have difficulty manipulating gear.

How deep are you? If you have practiced horizontal emergency ascents in a 25 m pool, you should be confident in your ability to ascend without air from a depth of 25 m (83 ft.) or less. You may ascend easily from farther down if you do not delay your start. You

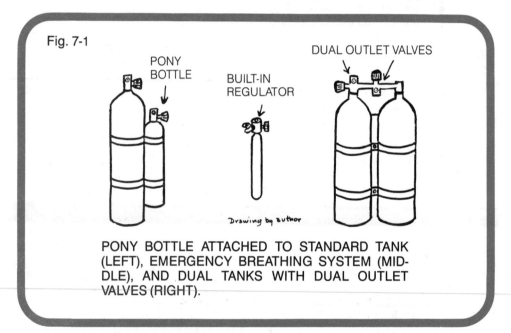

Fig. 7-1

PONY BOTTLE ATTACHED TO STANDARD TANK (LEFT), EMERGENCY BREATHING SYSTEM (MIDDLE), AND DUAL TANKS WITH DUAL OUTLET VALVES (RIGHT).

Equipment available

Your problems are minimized if your buddy has dual tanks with dual regulators, a small bailout bottle with a built-in regulator, or a pony bottle, preferably detachable (but secure enough to avoid accidental loss) to allow independent action. But are you both familiar with this gear? You should have checked it out before entering the water or, better yet, practiced with it on earlier dives. Bailout bottles hold only a few breaths of air.

probably did not realize that you were experiencing a loss of air supply emergency until you exhaled, attempted to inhale and are now operating on your last breath. Do you take off for the surface alone (independent action) or do you solicit help (dependent action)?

Extra second stages

You may decide to depend on your buddy. Ideally, your buddy is watching, is within arm's reach, knows what to do and has a spare regulator second stage (octopus) with *plenty of air to share*. If the spare regulator is attached to a pony bottle, so much the better. A separate air supply avoids the possibility of over-breathing or a freeze-up and reduces the possibility of both buddies running out of air again.

Rescue of others

Some instructors recommend offering the regulator through which you are breathing, using the spare second stage for yourself. Others claim it is best to offer the victim your spare second stage. The rationale for giving a victim your primary regulator is as follows:

In stress situations peripheral vision narrows. The out-of-air diver is probably thinking of only one thing, *air*! The regulator he sees in your mouth producing all those vital bubbles is obviously working. His experience with buddy breathing will lead him toward it. If you try to hand him your spare second stage he may not recognize it as a regulator. The arrangement of spare regulator hoses is not standardized. When mounted on the tank they point in different directions, with the second stages attached in random spots or simply left to dangle. The

regulator in the rescuer's mouth can be handed over quickly. It may take a while to locate the spare.

Those who recommend offering the victim the spare regulator use the following arguments: Statistics indicate that a hazard is created any time a regulator is removed from the mouth. As the rescuer you could easily have trouble finding or operating your second stage. Suddenly you've got to rescue yourself as well as the victim. In addition, the octopus regulator hose is normally made about ten inches longer than the standard hose, so that another diver can use it easily. If you don't let the victim have the long hose, you are failing to enlist a potentially important advantage.

One answer to this primary versus spare dilemma might be to anticipate giving air (if possible): switch regulators, and breathe through the long-hose regulator just prior to handing it to the victim. He will accept it eagerly because it is obviously working. The primary regulator stays in your hand during the switch so it can be easily replaced. Another answer is to use the regulator with the long-hose as your primary source.

Whichever method is used, most agree that the best location for the spare second stage is

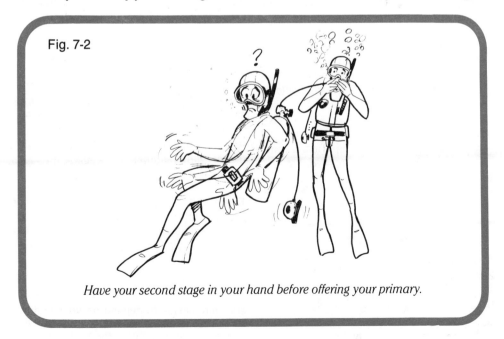

Fig. 7-2

Have your second stage in your hand before offering your primary.

on the diver's chest where it is readily accessible. Use an attachment that releases quickly and easily. Clearly identify your *pony* regulator so you don't accidentally use it for normal breathing. Color it or remove the exhaust "T".

Most divers have tried buddy breathing once or twice in a calm, clear, warm swimming pool, unencumbered by wet suits or neoprene gloves. Most never practiced again. Yet it takes at least seventeen practice exposures to perform buddy breathing effectively in a

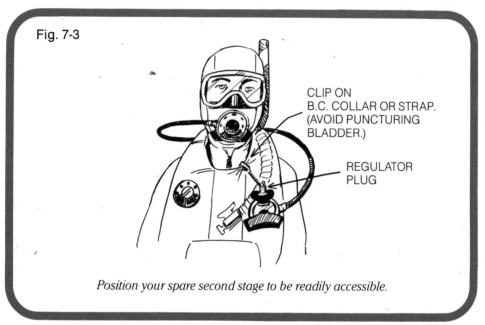

Fig. 7-3

CLIP ON
B.C. COLLAR OR STRAP.
(AVOID PUNCTURING
BLADDER.)

REGULATOR
PLUG

Position your spare second stage to be readily accessible.

Once you initiate breathing through separate stages, your ascent should be delayed long enough for you both to gain composure. Streaking for the surface while panicky or air-hungry could be disastrous. Keep thinking. How much air remains in the rescuer's tank? If a pony bottle is being used, remember that it is for emergencies only; it doesn't contain very much air. If the water is cold, below 5°C (42°F) and you are deep, the extra-heavy air-flow through the first stage of an octopus regulator may cause a freeze-up. Taking your breaths in turn will help to avoid over-breathing the octopus.

Buddy breathing

A second dependent action, much less desirable than using spare air, is buddy breathing. Victim and rescuer pass the same regulator back and forth, breathing alternately. Statistics however, show that in an emergency buddy breathers frequently die. Why?

real emergency. In open water with full gear it is not so easily done, especially when you are sharing air with an uptight diver who has never practiced with you.

Whenever the regulator is removed, the potential for trouble increases. Regular breathing is interrupted. A few drops of water inadvertently inhaled may cause a coughing spell or laryngeal spasm. Also, the pressure to pass the regulator quickly may cause stress. Breathing slowly and carefully will reduce the likelihood of strangling. Practice will reduce the probability of panic.

To be sure you have him when you need him, don't let your buddy get more than an arm's length away. If your air stops you may do best to surface via an emergency ascent. Avoid the necessity by staying close together, watching each other and monitoring both air supplies. If you are physically similar, when you run out of air, his supply will be gone soon, too. Monitor your air gauge. When you and your buddy breathe, the tank will naturally be depleted twice as quickly—or faster still, if one of you is air-hungry.

In a panic situation a diver may require as much as 350 litres (12 cubic feet) of air per minute, a demand beyond the operational capability of most regulators when tank pressure is below 300 or 400 psi (22-29 kg/cm²).[1]

As with extra second stage breathing, delay your ascent long enough to gain composure. Once you have established a rhythm and dispelled panic, ascend immediately—at the normal rate of 18 m (60 ft.)/min.

Regulator clearing

You exhaled too much with your last breath and now you don't have enough air to clear the regulator your buddy is holding. He is gripping it tightly, to keep you from stealing it, but he is also covering the purge valve with his palm! How can you get rid of the water and start breathing again?

Self-rescue

No need to panic or swallow the water. Fill your cheeks from the flooded mouthpiece, then expel the water through the exhaust ports. Repeating this a few times will eliminate all the water. Another method is to bubble air through the water. If you suck the water into your mouth slowly you will eventually get air bubbling through. Breathe that air carefully. A fast inhalation may cause a coughing spell. Exhaling it will clear the regulator for your next breath. This method works best when the mouthpiece is not completely full of water. Experienced divers normally breathe this way to avoid strangling from stray water in a regulator or snorkel. Other methods of clearing a regulator are to cough the water out, or push it out with your tongue.

If you are using a two-hose regulator, clear the mouthpiece by aiming it down and holding it higher than the regulator. It will free-flow and push the water out. If you keep the mouthpiece aimed down, no water will enter.

There's a less well known way of clearing a two-hose: milk the intake hose (the one on the right), thereby pushing air into the mouthpiece and forcing the water out.

Failure to properly clear a regulator, an oversight that typically leads to coughing and laryngeal spasms, is probably one of the main causes of scuba accidents during buddy breathing.

Rescue of others

When passing a single hose regulator for buddy breathing, habitually keep the purge button unobstructed. Either hold the regulator at the base (near the hose), or spread your fingers to allow access to the purge button between them. Keeping the mouthpiece aimed down as you exchange reduces the necessity for clearing.

As an air donor, you should be in complete control. Hold the victim on your left with one hand and grip your regulator tightly (leaving the purge button free) with the other. Unless the victim is very weak, don't try to guide the regulator to his mouth. He'll be able to do that better than you, even if he can't see.

Form the correct habit. Forgetting to vent air while the buddy has the regulator is probably another major cause of buddy breathing accidents. Since you need some air to purge a regulator in the normal way, don't empty your lungs completely between breaths. This could lead to a low volume embolism. Exhale slowly and gently. As long as you keep the airway open, any pressure building in your lungs will equalize. (See "Lung Ruptures" in next chapter.)

Placing the regulator between your lips and teeth is not necessary when buddy breathing. With practice, you will find that you can get air a lot faster by simply pressing the flange against your lips.

Before offering your regulator to an air-hungry diver, be sure you have a reserve for

[1]Emergency Ascent Training, *the fifteenth Undersea Medical Society Workshop, Bethesda, Maryland, December, 1977. UMS publication No. 32, W.S. (EAT) December 31, 1979, page 16.*

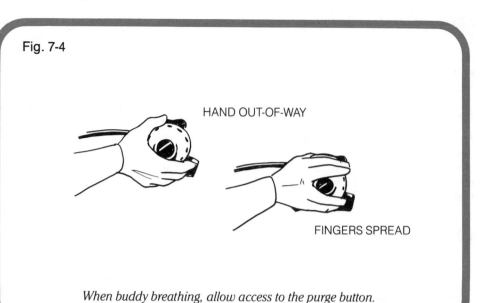

Fig. 7-4

HAND OUT-OF-WAY

FINGERS SPREAD

When buddy breathing, allow access to the purge button.

yourself. Take an extra breath if necessary. Remember, you may not get your regulator back. Many instructors recommend that the rescuer never remove his hand from his regulator. If the victim hogs the regulator, you have only a few choices. If you wait until he is satiated, you may suffer serious air-hunger yourself. You might try an emergency swimming ascent, taking him with you. Or, you might try to get the regulator back.

One way to retrieve your regulator is to grasp it and rapidly rotate your hand, twisting the top of the regulator in and down toward the victim's lower lip. Swift action is essential for its surprise effect.

Another method is to grasp the regulator and

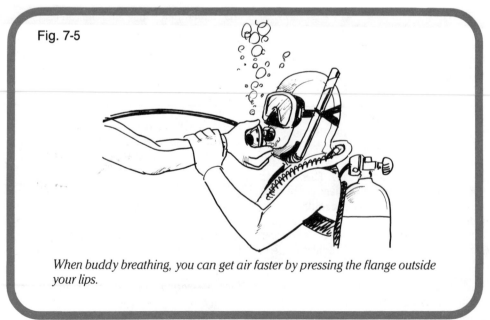

Fig. 7-5

When buddy breathing, you can get air faster by pressing the flange outside your lips.

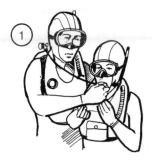
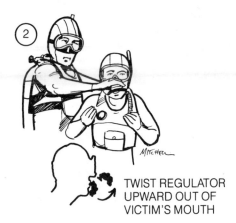

Fig. 7-6

TWIST REGULATOR
UPWARD OUT OF
VICTIM'S MOUTH

A swift twist down and in against victim's thumbs will loosen his grasp on your regulator.

bring your feet up against the victim's body. Straighten your knees and you will pull the regulator away.

With either method, the retrieved regulator may look odd. The rubber mouthpiece may have remained in the victim's mouth! But the regulator will still work. Just breathe through the open metal end.

Remember that any extra exertion, especially at depth, when low on air, can cause you to over-breathe your regulator. If your struggle is strenuous and prolonged, neither of you will get enough air.

For a method that avoids exertion, see "Breathing From a Buoyancy Compensator" later in this chapter.

Fig. 7-7

Straightening your legs against the victim's chest allows you to retrieve a hogged regulator.

Emergency swimming ascents

Many divers feel strongly that it is best not to depend upon someone else to rescue you when you are out of air. Do not be surprised if your buddy decides not to share his precious air. He may back-pedal away and desert you!

Self-rescue

After an almost instantaneous consideration of all the factors involved, you may decide to make an emergency swimming ascent, venting air all the way. Ascend as close to normal speed as you can knowing your own limits, looking toward the surface with one arm held high.

Keep your regulator in your mouth. The air in your "empty" tank may expand enough to let you suck in a breath or two on the way up. Unfortunately, your glottis tends to close automatically when you are not breathing. However, it will stay open if you exhale or try to inhale. Therefore, go through the motions of breathing even when you know there is no air—another reason for keeping your regulator in your mouth. (If your regulator is out,

attempt to inhale against closed lips. Pressing the side of your hand against your mouth will make this easier.) Refrain from swallowing. When you swallow, the glottis seals and allows air pressure to build as you rise. This may over-expand and rupture your lungs. Or, the increased pressure in your chest may slow the return of venous blood to the heart resulting in unconsciousness.

Psychological factors can complicate an ascent—lack of confidence, confusion resulting from murky water, pressure of an emergency situation. Maybe you couldn't get a full breath before leaving for the surface. Almost empty lungs will increase your air hunger. Inhaling against a dry regulator or closed lips will keep your glottis open and allow your lungs to partially inflate, reducing your air hunger. Alternately, exhale and then try to inhale. There is no need to increase the rate of this cycle if you ascend more rapidly. Any excess air will expel on its own if you don't hold your breath, ie, break the ventilator cycle.

According to a number of accident reports, divers have ruptured their lungs even while "doing everything right" (exhaling, humming, or singing to vent air while rising).

Fig. 7-8

Flare out to slow your ascent as you approach the surface.

Recent research indicates that these methods may be dangerous. Exhaling too little, or resisting airflow by humming or singing, may allow over-expansion of lung tissue. Exhaling too much or too fast may reduce lung volume and cause minute airways to collapse and trap air thereby allowing portions of the lung to over-expand and rupture. Obviously, don't blow and go.

All ascents should be performed as close to a normal ascent as is possible. Breathe, or attempt to breathe, all the way up and maintain a 18 m (60 ft.) min. rate.

If at this rate you are in danger of blacking out before surfacing, go faster. If necessary, ditch your weights and inflate your BC. A case of the bends is preferable to drowning due to a blackout from lack of oxygen. The deeper you are when you run out of air the more time it takes to get to the surface. Make the judgment to surface quickly and start moving up.

It is always a good idea to have some air in your BC when nearing the surface because if you are going to blackout, this is where it will occur. The air in your BC will ensure that you are brought to the surface and also should maintain your face out of the water should you lose consciousness. You can slow your ascent by flaring.

Rescue of others

If your buddy suddenly streaks for the surface *and you see no exhaled bubbles*, you may be able to stop him by grabbing his legs or his fins. If the fins come off in your hands, he will not be able to swim up as fast.

But should you stop him? A study has shown that when a rescuer attempts to stop an out-of-air victim, the rescuer frequently holds *his* breath. He may risk a lung rupture if the victim drags him up.

If you are certain you can stop the victim without forgetting to vent air, grip him strongly, look him sternly in the eye and signal him to exhale. Do not punch or squeeze the victim's chest to make him exhale. The force of a punch could cause the air embolism you are trying to prevent. Squeez-

ing his chest could inhibit him from inhaling residual air. Both may result in other problems.

Buoyant ascents

Fully buoyant ascents are inherently dangerous due to your high velocity near the surface. At fast speeds, even a slight restriction in your airflow can result in over expansion and rupture your lungs. Such restrictions may be caused by scar tissue, or by excess mucous or congestion as a result of smoking or a respiratory illness.

Self-rescue

Accordingly, aim for moderate buoyancy and be prepared to control your speed through shallow water by venting BC air or by flaring. To control a buoyant ascent with your BC, raise the hose to the level where the bubbles escape, raise the hose to slow ascent, or lower it to speed up.

Blacking out underwater is obviously dangerous. If you have any symptoms of impending blackout—euphoria, tingling, weakness, tunnel vision, dizziness, clumsiness, confusion—or you doubt your ability to surface while still conscious, make yourself fully buoyant.

If you blackout, your muscles will probably relax and you will vent the excess air automatically. At the surface, your fully-inflated buoyancy compensator will probably lift your chest clear of the water, so you will get an involuntary breath before falling back—face-up, if your BC is designed correctly.

Tests have shown that you are more likely to arrive at the surface in a face-up position, breathing despite unconsciousness, if you can manage to do two things prior to blacking out.[2] First, after making yourself buoyant, arch your back. This will help you to ascend face-up. Second, if you are in a face-down position underwater, raise one elbow above the horizontal plane of your shoulder, as if you were starting a crawl stroke. This procedure, called the raised elbow technique, produces a torque and an unequal buoyancy whereby your vest rolls you face-up.

[2]*John Ratliff, "The Life Vest,"* Proceedings of the 6th International Conference on Underwater Education *(IQ₆),* October, 1974, San Diego, California, NAUI, 1975, page 317.

Fig. 7-9

If you feel impending blackout underwater, arching your back and raising one elbow will help you to arrive face-up on the surface, breathing despite unconsciousness.

Breathing from a buoyancy compensator

Many divers have saved themselves and others by using a buoyancy compensator as an emergency source of breathable air.

Self-rescue

If your BC was inflated from your tank during your dive the air will be fresh. Air previously blown, or exhaled from your lungs will not be fresh, but it will be breathable. It will contain less oxygen and more carbon dioxide. But remember, we use exhaled air for artificial respiration, so it should be all right to re-breathe. At 33 metres (100 ft.) it will have four times as many molecules of oxygen. Re-breathing will make this O_2 available rather than wasting it in the open water.

Obviously, if you continue to re-breathe that same air, each breath will contain less oxygen and more carbon dioxide until you reach the point where it will no longer satisfy your increasing hunger for fresh air. The breakpoint will be surprisingly long in coming. By inflating and deflating your lungs you are stimulating stretch receptors in your chest, thereby partially relieving your air hunger.

You are also using the oxygen that is in the dead space of your airways and not in contact with the alveoli where the exchange of gases takes place. You will probably find that you can re-breathe eight to thirteen times without becoming air hungry. As the carbon dioxide builds up, you'll breathe faster and faster. It is possible to re-breathe over forty breaths this way—plenty to get you to the surface.

Getting air is the obvious advantage of BC re-breathing. It also keeps you from holding your breath and closing your airway. Any pressure differences between the air in your lungs and the surrounding water will automatically equalize.

The deeper you are at the start of an ascent, the more air you will have at your disposal (four times its original volume from 33 metres). This extra air will increase your buoyancy, especially as you near the surface. You may need to exhale through your nose to avoid an uncontrolled ascent. A large purge valve in your mask will make exhaling easy. If you have no purge valve, air will escape around the edges of the mask skirt.

Partially inflated, the BC acts as an extra-large second stage regulator diaphragm, allowing you to breathe easily at the pressure of the surrounding water. However, fully inflated, the BC will no longer flex. It will act as a rigid container and allow the air pressure to exceed the water pressure. Breathing this air could possibly rupture your lungs. Therefore, don't breathe from a fully inflated BC. Avoid this by not allowing your BC to inflate completely. Keep it from over-filling by exhaling through your nose.

Fresh air from the BC

One strategy is to exhale only your first breath into the BC. It will be the richest in oxygen and will expand as you rise. If you vent your subsequent exhalations into open water, you will be inhaling relatively fresh air all the way up.

If your second stage fails and you have an automatic tank air inflator, you can feed air into your BC from the first stage and breathe fresh air from the BC.

Rescue of others

Again with the tank inflator, you can use your BC as an extra second stage regulator. This is in effect "a poor man's octopus". You can give your regulator to an air-starved buddy and breathe the completely fresh air being fed into your BC. (Exhale through your nose.) Both you and your buddy can breathe fresh air this way for as long as your tank has air. This technique has worked in at least four actual emergencies as deep as one hundred feet.[3]

Self-rescue

If your BC uses a small air bottle for inflation, you have, in effect, a "poor man's pony bottle". It can be a source of *fresh* air for *you* if your tank runs dry or your regulator malfunctions.

A tank inflator hose or small air bottle inflator can be crucial if you find yourself low on air while exploring a wreck or cave. You can conserve air by re-breathing batches, feeding yourself fresh air intermittently.

Build your confidence by practicing BC breathing in a pool. It can be tricky. You need to clear the mouthpiece so you don't accidentally inhale water. The small amount that collects in most mouthpieces can be easily purged, or drained into the vest.

Many BCs have small purge openings in the tip of the mouthpiece, right under the filler button. This type of mouthpiece can be cleared by aiming the tip end down so the water will run out as you blow. Continue blowing as you push the filler button. The air will enter the BC, the holes will be sealed and the water will not return. Don't release the button or water will run back in through the holes.

Fig. 7-10

OUT-OF-AIR BUDDY BREATHING FROM REGULATOR ATTACHED TO THIS TANK

EXHALING THROUGH NOSE

BREATHING FRESH AIR FROM BC

FEEDING FRESH AIR INTO BC INTERMITTENTLY

Your BC can serve as a "poor man's octopus".

[3]*Dave Woodward, Letter to* NAUI News, *July, 1973, page 11.*

Fig. 7-11

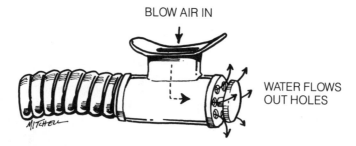

BLOW AIR IN

WATER FLOWS
OUT HOLES

This type of mouthpiece can be cleared by aiming it down and pushing the button as you blow into the BC.

Most other mouthpiece types (the kind that have no holes) can be cleared by the following method. These four steps work also for the mouthpieces with purge openings.

1. Seal your lips over the mouthpiece. Look down as you push the valve open, then blow the water that is in the mouthpiece into the hose.

2. Rotate your body in the direction the hose end is pointing (Picture the mouthpiece as an arrowhead.) Water will roll from the hose into the bottom of the BC. You should be looking toward the surface as you complete this roll. Blowing as you roll will help to clear small water drops from the hose corrugations.

Fig. 7-12 *Other mouthpieces can be cleared by blowing as you roll.*

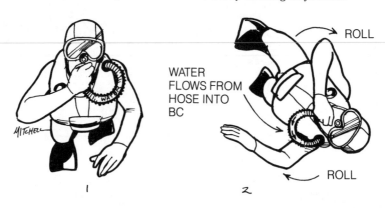

WATER FLOWS FROM HOSE INTO BC

ROLL

ROLL

As you roll the water in the hose will drain into the bottom of the BC.

Mitchell drawings reproduced with permission from "Your Buoyancy Compensator, an Emergency Source of Breathable Air" by the author in Proceedings of IQ11.

3. Inhale cautiously at first to be sure you are not getting water, then inhale more fully.

4. Keep your mouth sealed, the valve open, and your head up as you ascend. If you remove the inflator from your mouth, you'll have to clear it again. You can't let go of the inflator valve without shutting off your air. If you release the button of a perforated BC mouthpiece, you may find yourself inhaling water. Firm pressure is needed to keep such a mouthpiece from leaking water.

Precautions

In breathing from a buoyancy compensator, some problems can develop. However, they are all avoidable.

- If stray droplets cause a coughing spell, do not remove your mouth. Cough into the BC. That air will then be there to re-breathe when you have cleared your throat.

- The major disadvantage of BC re-breathing, as opposed to the emergency ascent, is that you have to remove your regulator from your mouth. This would seem to eliminate the possibility of breathing tank air as it becomes available and useful through expansion. However, this residual air will not leave the tank and will stay fresh. You can switch back to your regulator later and breathe that fresh air as you approach the surface when you need air most. Or, if you have an inflator hose from your tank, holding that control valve open will allow such residual air to flow into the BC and raise the percentage of oxygen in the air being breathed.

- You may forget to eliminate all the carbon dioxide after inflating the BC from a cartridge. One full breath of 100% CO_2 may do you in. This is not likely, however. Pure carbon dioxide is so stingingly pungent you'll probably stop after only a slight taste. Avoid this problem by habitually flushing out all traces of CO_2 immediately after each cartridge inflation has served its purpose.

- There is a possibility of bacterial or fungus infection from a contaminated BC. Clean out your BC prior to practice in breathing from it, with well-chlorinated swimming pool water followed by tap water. To be more certain, pour in a solution of benzalkonium chloride and swish it around, intermittently for a half hour. This will kill bacteria and fungi, and will not harm the bladder of the BC. Drug stores sell the concentrate under the brand names Zephiran Chloride® and Roccal®. Dilute it according to directions. After treating the BC, thoroughly rinse it out with tap water. Avoid contact with eyes and clothes. Flush away any solution which spills on the skin.

- Controlling your buoyancy may be a problem. However, you are likely to use BC breathing only when you are very deep. You will have time to grow accustomed to adjusting your rate of ascent before reaching the shallows. If your BC has no source of air except your own breath, you can slow your ascent by exhaling through your nose or by flaring out. If your BC has an air source which you are using as a spare regulator, you can control your buoyancy and still get enough breaths by feeding air into the BC intermittently and exhaling through your nose. Depending on the position and operation of your inflator controls, finding the right balance may be easy or difficult. Some air-bottle inflators require two hands. Practice is essential.

- Some divers fear blacking out on the way up as a result of diminished oxygen in the BC. However, in BC re-breathing, you are using up all the available oxygen instead of exhaling it into the open water. A more likely possibility is an underwater blackout while practicing in a pool. To prevent this, have someone watch you. He should be instructed to pull you out if, while re-breathing, you stay under longer than two minutes.

- Two divers drawing air at the same time may overbreathe the first stage of the regulator. This is even more likely if three divers are breathing fresh air—one from the primary, one from the octopus, and one from a BC, via the low-pressure inflator hose. Some regulators that furnish air with very little resistance at the start of a dive are "hard breathers" for a working diver at depth, with low tank air pressure. (The type regulator that is integral with the BC oral inflator hose has a high breathing resistance.) The air flow through the first stage (and correspondingly the breathing resistance) can be reduced by alternating breaths through the second stages (primary and octopus) and by feeding air into the BC between such inhalations. However, you can breathe the air that is already in the BC at any time without increasing the flow through the first stage. Also, BC breathing is always easy. There is very little resistance regardless of depth,

exertion, or low air pressure.

All of this available air should give you confidence. You won't be tempted to rush for the surface the moment that you realize you are out of air. You can breathe from your BC, take it easy, and swim leisurely to the surface.

Continual monitoring of submersible pressure gauges—your's and your fellow diver's—is obviously the best way to prevent air loss. Unfortunately, respiratory problems underwater may cause so much stress that a diver will fail to check his gauge or heed the warning of an audible alarm.

Summary

Loss of air supply

Lack of air leads quickly to a high-stress, high-risk situation both for the diver affected and his buddy. The thoroughness of training and the frequency of practice sessions involving loss of air supply situations will determine the diver's ability to cope with and resolve this major emergency situation.

Successful self-rescue

Ability depends on the adequacy of the diver's preparation, especially knowledge of his own equipment and practice in switching to emergency supplies of air.

Of particular importance with respect to the rescue of others in this situation, is the ability to exercise good judgment quickly in terms of selecting the best alternative available under the circumstances. The intelligent diver will ALWAYS SELECT THE COURSE OF ACTION, WHICH WILL SOLVE THE VICTIM'S PROBLEM, WITH THE LOWEST DEGREE OF RISK TO THE RESCUER.

CHAPTER 8

Respiratory problems

Erratic breathing

Scuba divers breathe almost entirely in and out through the mouth. Exhalation through the nose usually occurs only to equalize pressure or to clear the face mask. The mask normally prevents nasal inhalations. If your mask leaks or if it is knocked off, you could inhale water. The best prevention of a resulting laryngeal spasm is a strongly formed habit of inhaling only by mouth whenever your nose is exposed to the water.

Slow, deep breaths are considered the most efficient for the usual dive. Whenever you are not inhaling you should be exhaling. Holding a breath is appropriate only when necessary for the task at hand, for example, stalking or photographing a fish. During such breath holds, avoid lung rupture by making sure that your lungs are not filled to capacity, that there are no high waves over head, and that you are not moving upward.

Coughing

A coughing diver, struggling to stay afloat, may be losing buoyancy each time he coughs out air and gets none back.

Self-rescue

If you need to cough when at the surface, try submerging your face. In the water, your head will weigh almost nothing and you can cough underwater easily. By aiming your mouth down, you are allowing gravity to help expel the water. Stay near the surface so you can lift your head to breathe as soon as the coughing spell is over. Practice coughing in standing depth water until you build your confidence.

During a dive, water in your regulator could cause a coughing spell. The experienced diver will sense the presence of water in the air passages, and will breathe slowly and cautiously, thereby minimizing the possibility of a laryngeal spasm and coughing spell. Swallowing may help to eliminate stray droplets. If you do start coughing you can do it through your regulator. Keep the exhalation port aimed down to expel the water.

You can sharply reduce the likelihood of any lung rupture accident if you never *fully* inflate your lungs. Give yourself a margin for error. Alveoli must expand fully before they leak air.

Rescue of others

A coughing diver, whether underwater or on

Fig. 8-1

A coughing diver is losing buoyancy and may need help.

the surface, could be in trouble. Get to him quickly and give assistance if needed. Underwater, a coughing diver may rush to the surface. Follow him up at a slower pace and check on the surface to make sure he hasn't ruptured lung tissue. If a diver starts coughing on the surface, a little support may be all he needs so he can calm down and clear his air passages. Make yourself buoyant first.

Exertion breathing

Most regulators will not adequately support even moderately heavy respiratory work at 40 m (130 ft.) when the tank air is below 22 kg per cm² (300 psi). Some regulators won't give adequate air to a working diver down only 20 m (66 ft.). Trying to inhale large gulps of air to satisfy the air hunger of exertion may start a vicious cycle. The more air you feel you need, the harder you work to get it. The harder you work, the more air you need. If you suck air through a regulator fast enough to double the flow, you will create four times the resistance and use eight times as much oxygen.

Self-rescue

If you are caught in an exertion breathing cycle, stop working, ascend, and breathe deeply.

Rescue of others

You may be able to stop your buddy if he gets into similar trouble. Signal him back if he goes too deep; slow him down if he starts strenuous activity; and signal him to surface when low on air. He may think he is out of air and want to buddy breathe. That will not help. If your tank pressure is the same as his, and both regulators have similar breathing characteristics, he'll be no better off. If you have more tank pressure, an easier-breathing regulator, or both, he is likely to keep your regulator.

If you are certain that your buddy is in an exertion breathing cycle, let him have your regulator and try his. If you are not so air hungry, you may be able to breathe from it easily. As you ascend, both regulators will deliver air more freely.

It may not help at all to give your buddy your octopus regulator. Two persons breathing through the first stage of the same regulator may over-breathe it especially if both inhale at the same time. Do not give an air-hungry diver a spare regulator that is a part of an oral hose BC inflator. That type breathes hard. He will be worse off. Also, the hose is so short he'll have trouble getting it to his mouth. If you give him your primary regulator and you use the oral hose type, it may help him, but you may not get enough air. If you don't alternate breaths, neither probably will. A pony bottle or BC breathing would help solve this dilemma, but prevention is best. Avoid exertion underwater, especially at depth with low tank pressure.

Panting

We have been discussing the type of rapid deep breathing similar to that which occurs after running a race. Rapid *shallow* breathing, however, is another problem. In this situation, inhalations do not get air as far as the alveoli (air sacs in which oxygen is exchanged for carbon dioxide).

In the airway "dead" spaces, the same air moves back and forth. In the lungs, carbon dioxide accumulates and oxygen is depleted. On the surface, your lack of buoyancy, due to the small volumes of air inhaled, makes you work harder to stay afloat. This, combined with the poor exchange of oxygen for carbon dioxide, increases air hunger, which in turn triggers more rapid breathing—another vicious cycle. Exhaustion and panic, if not already present, may soon follow.

Self-rescue

If you are panting, breathe deeply and stop strenuous activity. Make yourself buoyant by inflating your BC or dropping weights. If you can't do either, turn over onto your back.

Rescue of others

You can help such a diver by reducing his work load and getting him to breathe more deeply. Making him more buoyant will usually accomplish both.

Hyperventilation

Hyperventilation is the over ventilation of the lungs through deep, fast breaths. We have all been cautioned not to hyperventilate for more than a few breaths prior to a

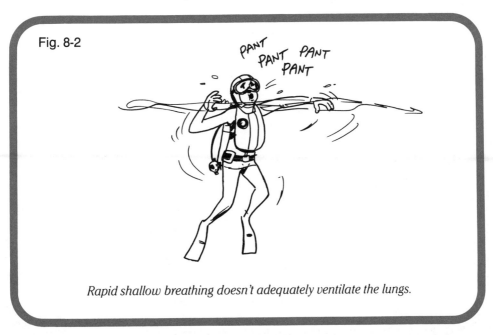

Fig. 8-2

Rapid shallow breathing doesn't adequately ventilate the lungs.

long breath-hold dive. Involuntary hyperventilation is another story. It is common during an apprehensive first open water dive.

The novice gulps deep fast breaths, over-filling his lungs and washing too much carbon dioxide from his body. Without enough CO_2, the body undergoes biochemical changes that increase nerve and muscle tension. A resulting tightness in the chest may be misinterpreted as shortness of breath. Frightened, the novice breathes more vigorously and another vicious cycle begins. The carbon dioxide drops to a dangerous level. Dizziness, panic, or blackout may follow.

Self-rescue

Hyperventilation is not likely seen in an experienced scuba diver. If you find yourself breathing too fast for the conditions, slow down. Long, slow exhalations will rebuild CO_2 levels.

Rescue of others

On showing signs of hyperventilation underwater, the diver should be signaled to slow down and exhale more deeply. If he persists, he should be brought to the surface, where the problem can be explained.

Inhaling without exhaling

Sometimes a novice diver under stress will find himself in another vicious cycle. He inhales fully, exhales only slightly, inhales fully again, exhales slightly, and so on. Feeling trapped underwater, he conserves his air at all costs. Each inhalation gets harder because pressure is building in his lungs. The cycle continues until he cannot inhale any further. Not understanding the problem, he assumes something is wrong with his regulator or his air supply. If he attempts to use another regulator, buddy breathing or extra second stage, the problem will naturally persist.

One sign of failure to exhale is that the diver appears unusually buoyant. There will be very few bubbles venting as he breathes. He may be kicking hard to stay down. Signal the diver to exhale and to take it easy.

Fig. 8-3

A novice diver may forget to breathe out. Signal him to exhale.

Skip breathing

Many divers, particularly experienced ones, pride themselves on their ability to stay underwater longer than anyone else. They may try to save air by skip breathing—inserting a long unnatural pause between each breath. It should be obvious that this is a dangerous practice.

Skip-breathers resist air-hunger signals. The resulting lack of oxygen and CO_2 build-up may cause confusion, headaches, drowsiness, and eventual loss of consciousness.

A skip-breather is also vulnerable to lung rupture. He may drift up unexpectedly during a 'breath hold'. Or a high wave may pass overhead, with the subsequent low trough reducing the pressure just as if he had drifted up.

A safer way to conserve air is to take it easy underwater. Prolong both inhalations and exhalations, but breathe in or out all of the time. Another way is to be in "tip-top" condition throughout the diving season. The better your physical fitness, the less air you will consume.

Exhaustion

Diver exhaustion continues to be a most common cause of scuba fatalities. Whenever diving ceases to be a pleasant, easy-going experience, whenever we start exerting ourselves, we are inviting trouble.

Exhaustion makes a diver more susceptible to hyperventilation, cramps, the bends, and inert gas narcosis. It invites blackout from low blood sugar (hypoglycemia), low oxygen (hypoxia), high carbon dioxide (hypercapnea), and excessive cold (hypothermia).

Clearly, when using scuba, one should avoid any work that could lead to exhaustion. Just swimming with all the gear is more tiring than you realize. Factors leading to exhaustion may be present long before a dive, for example: poor physical condition, overweight, smoking, excessive drinking, lack of sleep, and skipped breakfasts. On the dive itself, avoid:

— swimming in heavy surf, high waves, or strong currents.
— trying to catch up with a buddy who swims fast and doesn't look back.
— chasing an elusive fish.
— treading water furiously in order to breathe surface air.

Any of these actions, and others like them, may cause labored breathing, increasing weakness, mental fatigue, anxiety and panic.

Fig. 8-4

HAND ME YOUR BAG

Tell an exhausted diver you'll take his goodies for him. If they jeopardize your safety, ditch them.

Self-rescue

If you experience fatigue underwater, stop all activity and breathe deeply. Ascend to a shallower depth where breathing will be easier and your ability to work will be enhanced. If exertion is necessary underwater to save yourself or your buddy, conserve energy by alternating bursts of activity with frequent rest periods.

On the surface, buoyancy will probably solve the problem. Inflate the BC and drop weights. By jettisoning salvaged gear, bags of sealife, and other goodies before the weight belt, you free arms for swimming. Too often an exhausted diver "commits suicide" by giving up too soon. If you find yourself drained of energy, with your life at stake, keep going. You are capable of much more effort than you realize. When you reach the end of your rope—tie it in a knot and hang on! The longer you keep your body and wits active, the more likely you are to be rescued, or to rescue yourself. You have nothing to gain by quitting.

Rescue of others

A diver struggling to stay on the surface may not discard treasures simply because you say so. Ask him to hand them to you. This will free his arms for swimming support. Don't keep this gear and drown. Ditch it.

Get the victim floating on his back. This keeps his head in the water, where it weighs almost nothing.

When assisting an exhausted or nearly exhausted diver, be extremely careful in your approach. You don't want to expose yourself to danger. However, an exhausted diver is usually incapable of dangerous action. He is more likely to simply lag behind, become confused, and then silently drown. Passivity, indecision, vagueness, indifference to self-preservation, and apparent willingness to slip below the surface—these appear again and again in case narratives by witnesses to diver fatigue fatalities.

Try to spot exhaustion before it builds in either yourself and your diving buddy. If, following a dive, a fellow diver appears listless and unresponsive, position yourself so you can watch him continually all the way back to the boat or shore. He could simply disappear from view!

Do not neglect the rescuer who has towed the victim to the boat or shore. He has probably expended enormous amounts of energy. Help him out of the water and be ready to treat him for shock, fatigue and exposure.

Fig. 8-5

Don't neglect the poor rescuer.

Lung ruptures

Any unexplained distress upon surfacing indicates the possibility of pulmonary overpressure. Autopsies fail to show definite ruptures of lung tissue. Air may escape through pores in over-expanded alveoli without visible injury. However, since it is the misdirected air that causes problems rather than the way it leaves the lungs, the commonly used term "lung rupture" is being used to avoid stilted prose.

exhalation, the small airways in the lower lungs may collapse. The residual air behind these collapsed tubes becomes trapped. The expanding air during the ascent may escape through the lung tissue.

Self-rescue

Therefore, exhalation during a scuba emergency ascent should not be forceful. Keep your chest at a comfortable volume and allow the expanding air to flow out of its own

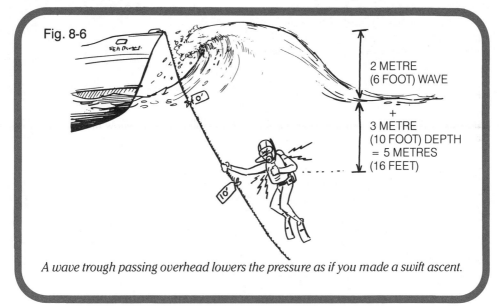

Fig. 8-6

2 METRE (6 FOOT) WAVE
+
3 METRE (10 FOOT) DEPTH
= 5 METRES (16 FEET)

A wave trough passing overhead lowers the pressure as if you made a swift ascent.

Due to rapid expansion of air near the surface, lung rupture is most likely to occur while rising through shallow water. However, it can also happen at depth. When sharing a regulator, if you take a full breath and hold it, rising from 18 to 15 m (60 to 50 ft.) while your buddy breathes, your lung tissue could rupture. You will have no problem however, if you have formed the habit of exhaling whenever you are not inhaling—whether you have a regulator in your mouth or not.

Inhaling while pushing the purge button, or swallowing while ascending (or even without ascending if high waves are overhead) can also cause lung rupture.

Recent research indicates that when blood pooling in the lungs (a normal diving response) is combined with a full or forceful

accord, alternately attempting to inhale through your regulator, or against closed lips.

Trapping of residual air can also be caused by small tumors or cysts, by the scarring deformities and secretions of chronic lung disease, by the small airway constriction of asthma, and by the swelling and thick mucous associated with acute infections and their aftermath. Swollen tissues or mucous in sufficient quantities to cause air embolism can last up to ten days after a severe cold. (Some say up to six weeks after a severe respiratory illness!) Regular physical examinations and even x-rays will not reveal most of these deficiencies. Smoking leaves your lungs less able to dispose of potentially dangerous mucous. And smoking could cause a coughing spell that starts trouble. You might reduce the risk of lung rupture by staying out of the water not only while you are ill, but for a long time afterwards. Lung obstructions are often partial rather than complete. If you ascend slowly, you may release enough air to avoid a rupture.

Rescue of others

While diving in 7-8m of water, your buddy, a heavy smoker, starts coughing, removes his regulator, claws rapidly upward and screams as he surfaces. You find him there, disoriented, confused, blue in the face and coughing a bloody froth— classic signs of air embolism. He could be blind or paralyzed. He could convulse or lose consciousness and stop breathing at any minute. He may panic from knowing he is seriously injured or act as if panicked due to a brain injury. He may simply sink and drown.

Get him back to the boat so he can be given first aid and transported to a hyperbaric chamber as soon as possible. A line from the boat will speed your progress. Call for help as you approach the victim. Exercise caution if he is panicky; do not expose yourself to unnecessary risks.

If he shows no signs of panic, remove his weight belt immediately and get him parallel to the surface for towing. Watch carefully, making sure he remains conscious and breathing. Be alert for possible vomiting or convulsions. If he loses consciousness, tilt his head back to keep his airway open.

Handling the victim from his left side may allow manipulation of his inflator hose as most are on the left. When draining vomit or performing mouth-to-mouth inflations, turn the victim's head and body to his left, assuming no waves are rushing forward from that direction.

Use the arm over arm tow, watch his face and be prepared to commence rescue breathing if necessary. If you switch to mouth-to-snorkel after a few breaths, you may get the victim more parallel to the surface and be able to tow him more easily.

Unless required for buoyant support, the first assistant on the scene should be directed to place the victim's feet on his shoulders, thereby elevating the victim's lower body. Direct other assisting divers to strip off the victim's tank and gear. You will want to remove him from the water unimpeded.

Anytime a diver makes an emergency or uncontrolled ascent, suspect a lung injury. Go to his aid immediately. Make him buoyant and check for abnormality—particularly loss of consciousness or respiratory arrest.

Summary

Causes of respiratory distress

The causes of respiratory distress are many and vary from minor, temporary irritants to major life-threatening situations. Many can be ascribed to diver stress of one sort or another.

Get the victim on the surface asap

The air supply itself is not the problem, but rather the inability of the diver to use it effectively. Thus the simple provision of air is not the solution. Persistent respiratory distress can only be relieved and resolved on the surface.

Other physiological problems

CHAPTER 9

Underwater blackout

We are familiar with many causes of unconsciousness—head injury, fainting, heart attack, stroke, hypothermia, alcohol, drugs, low blood sugar, venomous animals, or a too high or too low partial pressure of oxygen, nitrogen, carbon dioxide, or carbon monoxide, especially if it is in the wrong part of the body. But we may not be familiar with the following possible causes of blackout underwater:

Diving reflex

This reflex is a physiological oxygen-conserving mechanism triggered by breath-holding and by submerging the mouth and nostrils. The heart rate drops in consequence of oxygen-rich blood being re-routed from the gut and extremities to the heart and brain. The reflex is intensified by high CO_2, by fear, by high pressure, by water in the airways, by the valsalva maneuver (ear clearing by holding the nose and blowing) and, especially, by breath-holding with cold water on the face. A diver wearing a mask that is clear of water may fail to exhibit this reflex. This reflex helps aquatic animals and human beings, especially the young, to conserve oxygen and exist underwater longer. Although it is helpful in prolonging life, a study has revealed that the diving reflex can be a factor in blackouts. Normally the heart rate drops within the first twenty seconds of a breath-hold dive and stays lower than normal even if the research subject exercises. However, heart rate measurements of divers who could hold their breath beyond two

minutes revealed a second drop. This second drop can reduce the brain's oxygen supply and contribute to an underwater blackout.[1]

Such blackouts threaten breath-hold divers particularly. But remember, a scuba diver who runs out of air, very quickly becomes a breath-hold diver. The diver who skip breathes to conserve air is also vulnerable.

Rust

In the absence of carbon dioxide, there are no reliable symptoms that will warn you that you are not breathing oxygen. If the inside of a tank corrodes, the oxygen is used up in the process of combining with iron to form rust. Breathing almost pure nitrogen, you will blackout without warning.

Drain, inspect and refill tanks with fresh air after any long period of storage (six months or more). Steel tanks that contain moisture will rust internally depleting the amount of oxygen available in the air supply.

A similar oxygen depletion can occur inside a rusty wreck. If you remove your regulator to test an air pocket, the air may seem perfectly fresh. If you breathe it, however, you may blackout from insufficient oxygen.

[1]Dr. Alfred A. Bove, M.D., et al, "Diving Bradycardia as a Factor in Underwater Blackout," Aerospace Medicine, March, 1973.

Carotid sinus reflex

A wet suit or inflatable dry suit, may be so tight around the neck that it will cause a blackout from the carotid sinus reflex. The carotid arteries contain enlargements (sinuses) equipped with sensors that, by detecting blood pressure changes, ensure the brain an optimum flow of blood. When the pressure is too low, the heart is stimulated to pump harder. When the pressure is too high, the message will be for the heart to contract less frequently.

External pressure on these sinuses may trigger a false message so that blood pressure to the brain is lowered. The corresponding reduction could easily produce confusion, clumsiness and eventual blackout. Nerves near the surface in these areas, if massaged by movement of the neck under a tight collar, may slow the heart beat and cause similar problems. Sensitivity of the carotid sinus reflex is variable but greatly increases with age.

This problem can be avoided by making sure there is nothing tight around the neck, especially in the areas over the carotid sinuses as indicated by the illustration.

Self rescue

The symptoms of the approaching blackout are not at all reliable. They are so subtle that you as the victim are not likely to notice them. A changing heart rate may be a forewarning, but you would rarely be aware of that. Euphoria should be suspect because it frequently occurs before blackout; but feeling great is not normally associated with impending doom. Weakness, dizziness, confusion or clumsiness should tell you something is wrong, however, by that stage your brain may be so addled you are not likely to recognize any problem. If you do suspect a blackout, get buoyant in order that you float at the surface and can be found.

Rescue of others

As the victim's buddy you may detect his inappropriate behavior and abort the dive. An obvious clue to blackout is a diver slumping motionless especially if no air bubbles are coming out of his regulator.

Even if the bubbles are coming out at regular intervals, he could still be out cold. When in doubt, check.

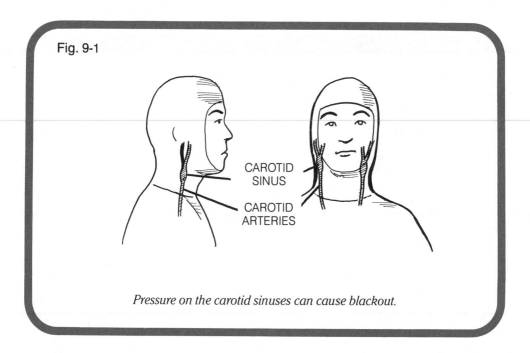

Fig. 9-1

CAROTID
SINUS

CAROTID
ARTERIES

Pressure on the carotid sinuses can cause blackout.

Massive bleeding

Life-threatening, major bleeding can be either bright red blood spurting from an artery or darker blood flowing from a large vein. Depending on your depth, blood may look green or black instead of red. Underwater, arterial blood will not spurt as it does on land but will form a diffused cloud in the water. Injuries underwater may not be painful at first and accordingly may not be noticed.

Rescue of self or others

Use direct pressure to stop the flow of blood. Swimming while holding a limb is difficult. If the distance is great, or if you are alone, consider using your gear to apply pressure. Your buoyancy compensator or inflatable vest might be used. It can be wrapped around a limb, fastened with its own straps, and inflated by mouth until the blood stops flowing. Its buoyancy will elevate the limb.

including those of the mouth and throat, which block air in the lungs. Surfacing rapidly could cause an air embolism.

Rescue of others

Controlling such a victim is not easy. Approach him from the rear, being careful that he does not knock away your regulator or mask. Do not restrain him any more than is necessary to prevent him from inhaling water. It *may* be possible also to help him as follows:

If the victim has not dropped his mouthpiece, hold it in. If clear, keep his mask on. If his regulator is not in his mouth, replace it. Then, with his chin on his chest and the exhalation ports aimed down, push the purge button. Since his throat is blocked, the mouthpiece will clear without water getting in his lungs. This will keep him from inhal-

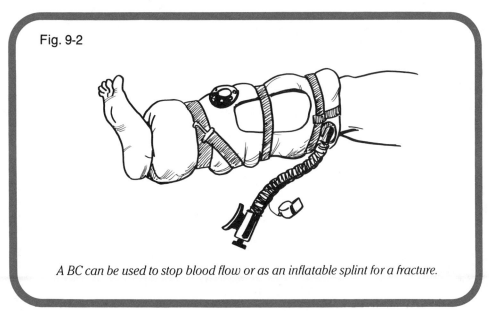

Fig. 9-2

A BC can be used to stop blood flow or as an inflatable splint for a fracture.

When all else fails to stop the blood, *and only then*, improvise a tourniquet, using wide gear straps. Tighten it by twisting with your knife sheath or spear gun.

Convulsions

Although a convulsing victim is unconscious, his muscles are contracting violently,

ing water and assure an air supply when he starts breathing.

While waiting for him to stop convulsing and start breathing, prepare to ascend. Check his gear so you can operate his BC and drop his weight belt quickly if needed. The victim may be passive, sleepy or semi-conscious as the spasms subside. Convulsions rarely last more than a minute or two. Going up, you must continue holding the regulator in his mouth with his head tilted back to keep the airway open.

Upon reaching the surface, remove the regulator and turn his head. Check breathing and establish buoyancy. Check the victim's regulator and inside his mouth to make sure that the nibs of the mouthpiece were not bitten off during the spasms. They could lodge in his throat.

If a victim starts convulsing on the surface, your primary job is to keep him from sinking or inhaling water. If you can do so without endangering yourself, make the victim buoyant with his face above water and head tilted back.

If the victim does not start breathing on his own after the spasms subside, initiate rescue breathing. The spasms may not have completely subsided, or they may recur, and the jaws may be clenched shut. If you cannot ventilate by parting his lips and blowing through the spaces between his teeth, try mouth-to-nose.

Decompression sickness (bends)

Decompression sickness is normally a result of bubbles of nitrogen in the blood or tissues due to inadequate decompression after diving deep and remaining longer than recommended by the tables. However, even if you calculate them carefully and do not confuse depths, times and residual nitrogen values, the tables may let you down. Bends have occurred in divers who have strictly followed the tables—even when not diving deeper than 10 m (33 ft.). Studies indicate that the no-decompression limits may be too liberal. In addition, the twelve hour surface interval to avoid repetitive dive calculation may be too short for some body tissues.

It isn't only the bubbles that cause the bends. It is also the clots that form around them. Clotting mechanisms are activated at the blood-bubble interface resulting in larger and stickier obstructions within the blood vessels.

Other factors which may make the bends more likely are: drugs, alcohol, strenuous exertions, obesity, age, cold water, deep bounce dives, skip breathing, illness, a run-down condition, insufficient rest, low fluid intake and inadequate food as well as high altitude during and after diving. Dependence upon an inaccurate timing device, faulty depth gauge or poorly designed decompression meter is also foolish. The surface is your last decompression stop. Avoid exercise on the boat or shore after diving.

Fig. 9-3

Joint pain is only one of many bends symptoms.

Symptoms of the bends

After any dive that approaches or exceeds no-decompression limits, question your buddy carefully to determine whether he might have any symptoms of decompression sickness. Look for pain, undue fatigue, muscle weakness, skin itch, numbness, or "pins and needles" feeling. In a serious case, there may be dizziness, loss of bowel or bladder control, nausea, vomiting, poor hearing, blurred vision, slurred speech, paralysis, or breathing difficulties. Other injuries may be confused with the bends. If squeezing the injury does not increase the pain, assume the cause is decompression sickness.

If he has *any* symptoms of decompression sickness, get him out of the water, apply first aid and arrange to transport him to a hyperbaric chamber. Never try to recompress the diver in the water. The successful treatment of bends requires many hours in a hyperbaric chamber attended by highly trained personnel making medical decisions based on symptoms.

The symptoms of the bends are frequently confused with those of air embolism. But bends symptoms are usually delayed, sometimes for hours, whereas air embolism symptoms normally appear within a very few minutes after surfacing. In view of this, if any such symptoms appear while the victim is still in the water, assume he has an air embolism.

Avoiding the bends

It is highly recommended that you always dive conservatively, adjusting your bottom time and depth in order that you never dive beyond the decompression limits. After every dive, rest for a few minutes at 3 m (10 ft.) below the surface before ascending.

One caution: At 3 m (10 ft.), some of your tissues may be loading up with nitrogen while others are unloading. Accordingly, your repetitive dive calculations for any subsequent dives may indicate insufficient values for residual nitrogen. To avoid this problem, use the total underwater time, including the time at 3 m (10 ft.), as if it was the bottom time, to obtain the residual nitrogen time.

If you are going in an aircraft after diving or if you are going to dive in fresh water above sea level, use special altitude diving procedures to avoid decompression sickness. New studies have indicated that procedures previously recommended for flying after diving or diving at high altitudes may be too liberal. These limits are now recommended:

After diving at sea level (without exceeding the U.S. Navy no-decompression limit) wait

Fig. 9-4

For extra safety, stop at 3 m (10 ft.) for a few minutes even if decompression is not needed.

at least twelve hours before flying above 900 m (approximately 3000 ft.).

Before diving at a high altitude (such as a mountain lake) wait at least twelve hours after you arrive. Then limit yourself to no-decompression diving using special no-decompression tables for each altitude where you dive.

Vomiting

A victim of near-drowning usually vomits at some point during rescue efforts. Expect it; don't let it throw you. Regurgitated stomach fluid looks bad, smells awful, feels slimy and tastes terrible. But it will not hurt you unless you inhale it. You wouldn't, but without protective reflexes, an unconscious victim is likely to inhale this fluid, causing extensive damage to his lungs. Position the victim in order to drain the vomit. If necessary, turn the victim's head away from you and sweep his mouth with your fingers.

Large particles and involuntary gasping may cause problems when a conscious diver vomits beneath the surface. Lumps may block the exhalation ports allowing vomitus to be inhaled on a subsequent breath. Or, lumps may become stuck in the exhaust valve, holding it open and allowing water to leak in. It would seem obvious that to avoid the lump problems the regulator should be removed from your mouth. However, an involuntary gasp while the regulator is removed could cause aspiration of much water into your lungs.

Self-rescue

In order to minimize these problems, face the bottom, press the purge button as you move the regulator to one corner of your mouth while keeping the other side open. The material, lumps and all, will be forced out the open side of your mouth and if you gasp, you will get air. With the regulator open to the water, you can safely hold the button down

until you are under control. After replacing and clearing the mouthpiece, inhale carefully to be certain you are breathing only air.

Rescue of others

An unconscious victim vomiting underwater presents a more difficult problem. While he is vomiting, he is necessarily holding his breath. If you rise with him, you could cause an air embolism. If he can vomit, he hasn't been out of air for long. So it will be safe to delay ascent. But be ready to take him up the moment he stops vomiting.

Cramps

Divers often get cramps in the calf of the leg and sometimes in the foot or thigh. Cramps are a painful contraction of the muscle caused when the muscle out-works its blood supply. Cramps are precipitated by cold water, sudden exertion, dehydration and sweating, ill-fitting fins, or the fatigue of excessive exercise, especially if the muscle is untrained. The resulting contraction can be violent and painful.

Self-rescue

Prior to a full locking contraction there usually will be a preliminary muscle twinge. If you are alert, you will recognize this sign and avoid the cramp by stretching the muscle.

A muscle locked in a tight contraction may be relieved by stretching. If the cramp is in the calf of your leg, pull the tip of that fin towards your shin as you straighten out your knee. You may need to rest this muscle to keep the cramp from returning. Inflate your vest. Use a different kick, then get out of the water if you can. Massaging the muscle may help.

Rescue of others

To assist a fellow diver who has a cramp, tell him or show him what to do. Unless a victim is completely unable to make any headway toward boat or shore, encourage him to return using a different kick. This will avoid the risk of a cramp of your own from the extra exertion of towing him. A ride back while being towed on a line would be ideal.

Nitrogen narcosis and uncontrolled descent

The narcotic effects of nitrogen may begin as shallow as 9 m (30 ft.). The probability of onset increases with depth, but serious mental degradation usually does not occur shallower than 30 m (100 ft.).

Nitrogen narcosis is potentiated by alcohol, fatigue, CO_2, ill health, apprehension, rapid compression, and hard work. There are wide variations of sensitivity among individuals.

The nitrogen-drugged diver may be elated, detached from reality, unable to concentrate, overconfident and giddy. A less well-known symptom is tingling numbness in the lips, gums and legs. At about 75 m (240 ft.), there may be stupor, hallucinations, awareness of impending blackout, the illusion of levitation, a loss of time sense, a dead-pan expression and eventual unconsciousness. Blackout has been observed to occur as shallow as 46 m (150 ft.).

Self-rescue

When you intend to dive deeply, set rigid limits on duration, depth and air consumption, and steel yourself to stick by them. Hard and fast decisions made ahead of time will help to overcome the influence of nitrogen narcosis. This is especially true of novices who may be more likely than veteran divers to experience silly, illogical, dangerous notions. One defense might be to recognize "the narcs" as an artificial high and to concentrate steadfastly on your purpose. A much better answer is to head for the surface if you have any of the symptoms. Ascending will decrease the effects, but you may have to go far, possibly even to the surface. Nitrogen narcosis that began at 76 m (250 ft.) may not be fully relieved until you reach 15 m (50 ft.). **A recommended prevention is for sport divers never to exceed 30 m (100 ft.).**

Rescue of others

Watch your buddy carefully for any signs of narcosis, especially foolish actions. For example, it is easy to exceed the planned limit when diving along the side of a wall, down a slope, terrace, through a wreck, inside a cave—in any situation where descent is not restricted by a continuous bottom. Stay close enough to your buddy that you can stop him if he becomes giddy and goes too deep. Grab him firmly by the arm, draw him up close, look him sternly in the eye and signal him to go up. If necessary, make him buoyant to the extent that he cannot help but ascend.

Fig. 9-5

Watch your buddy closely for signs of N_2 narcosis.

If you are not close enough to physically stop a diver who is going dangerously deep, bang on your tank or drop something in front of him to get his attention. Then motion him up.

increases rapidly. As you head for the surface with the victim, the divers above you may realize your predicament. They can provide breathing equipment, underwater decompression tables, ascent lines, and weight

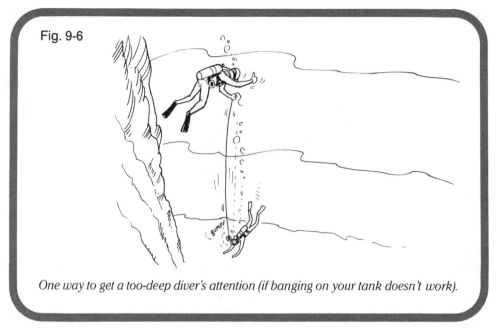

Fig. 9-6

One way to get a too-deep diver's attention (if banging on your tank doesn't work).

If he still continues down, obviously compromising his survival, should you go after him? Not unless you can avoid endangering your own life. Exercise enhances narcosis. A vigorous pursuit could leave you over-breathing your regulator with a dangerously low air supply and judgment as faulty as the victim's.

If you do go after the victim, handle him from the rear and immediately establish buoyancy for both of you. This may not be as easy as it seems. A CO_2 inflator, unless extra large, will not supply much buoyancy. Use a tank inflator. You will be too breathless to remove your regulator or inflate a BC orally. If you have no tank inflator, drop weight belts. However, due to wet suit compression, at depth, this will not necessarily afford much positive buoyancy. Also, in the clear, warm water of the tropics where this accident is most likely to happen, there may be no weight belt.

Care must be taken to avoid an uncontrolled *ascent*. Because you are deep, this is not an immediate problem; however, it will be as you hit the shallow water and your buoyancy

belts, enabling both you and the victim to decompress before surfacing. Even if you have yet to exceed your time at depth, stay at ten feet for awhile. You probably exerted yourself chasing the victim and are closer to the bends. It is unlikely that you checked either your time or depth during the rescue.

Horizontal disorientation

In mid-water or over a featureless bottom, it is easy to lose your sense of direction. One guideline is to note the direction of the current, though this may change at different levels and times. And often there is no current.

Self-rescue

On the bottom and in the absence of landmarks, sand ripples may orient a diver. The ripples are parallel to the waves that formed

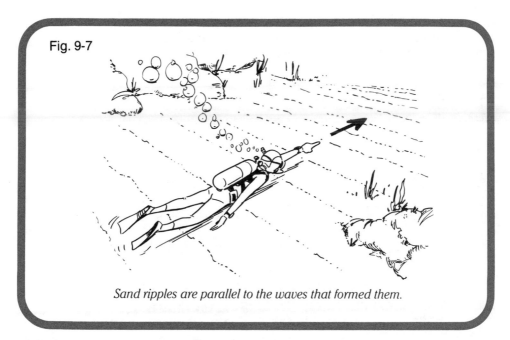

Fig. 9-7

Sand ripples are parallel to the waves that formed them.

them with the sharp crests pointing toward the shore.

If there are no bottom marks, you may make one with a knife, or by dragging an object. The mark will help you to find your way back. Be certain that the water's surge does not cover the trail behind you.

If the water is shallow enough to feel the surge, it will tell you the direction of the waves above. And near shore, the slope of the bottom usually points the way toward land.

A compass is useful but will be deflected severely by ferrous metal. Even if no wreck is near, a compass may lead you astray if you do not know how to use it.

Disorientation becomes a serious problem when you cannot come directly to the surface—in a wreck, in a cave, under ice or during saturation diving. An unsuspecting diver may blithely swim forward, believing he can safely go as far as he can see clearly. When he turns to go back however, the silt stirred up by his fins obstructs the view. Even with clear visibility it is easy to lose the way in the maze of passageways and blind alleys that characterize caves and wrecks. A guide line and training in its use is mandatory.

Vertical disorientation

Underwater disorientation may become so extreme that you swim toward the bottom when you think you are swimming up! One reason is that your most reliable indicator of orientation—gravity—has been lost. The water buoys you up so evenly that you feel weightless.

Underwater, fluid in the semi-circular canals of the ear can be set in motion even though the head is not turning. If an eardrum ruptures, cold water enters the middle ear and sets up convection currents in the semi-circular canals. Vertigo frequently results. It feels as if the world is spinning, and you grow nauseous.

But eardrum rupture is not the only event that can cause the canal fluid to move and give a misleading signal. Some of the chill of icy water in the outer ear canal is transmitted through an intact eardrum to the air in the middle ear, cooling the adjacent semi-circular canal fluid. If both ears are equally cold, the resulting convection currents will be equal and opposite so they cancel each other out. However, if cold water enters one ear and not the other, unequal convection currents will result, and the signals that reach the brain will be falsely interpreted as bodily rotation. Causes of this unequal cooling include: a skewed wet suit hood (uncovering one ear and not the other), excess wax in one ear, bony overgrowth in an ear canal wall, and swelling or fluid from infection.

Pressure differences between the left and right middle ear cavities can also cause vertigo. This often happens during fast vertical movement through the water, especially among divers who had trouble clearing one ear. Avoid this by slowing your ascents and descents. Stop and backtrack if necessary.

Ears also have sensing organs called utricles that tell us which way is up. They are most accurate when the head is initially vertical. Because we are rarely vertical when diving, and because the utricle's signals are weak, this organ is commonly overruled by bogus signals. Dizziness results. Descend feet first to minimize this problem.

Other causes of dizziness are nitrogen narcosis, dehydration, low blood sugar, drugs, illness, too much oxygen, too little oxygen, too much carbon dioxide (from skip breathing, for instance), and too little carbon dioxide (from hyperventilation).

Air embolism and decompression sickness can also cause dizziness, although the onset usually occurs after the diver has surfaced. The cause can be an injury to the brain or more likely to the ear. The ears are more susceptible to the bends than are most other parts of the body. If dizziness or deafness occurs during or after ascent, suspect decompression sickness. Any diver whose dizziness does not subside should be taken to a hyperbaric chamber for a medical examination and possible recompression.

Self-rescue

If you become disoriented, stop, breathe, and think. If you panic, you will probably do the wrong thing. Keep in mind that you have air. Hold on to a fixed object—a rock, an anchor line, or even, if it is hospitable and shallow, the bottom. In mid-water, hold your buddy and twirl circles with your finger near your head. He will probably take you up. Hug yourself if your buddy is not close. In such an emergency you are liable to hold your breath. Breathe. If you drift up, you could embolize.

Did cold water in one ear cause your vertigo? It will probably subside within a minute as the water in your ear warms up. If you close your eyes and relax, your body will normally begin rotating to a head-up position, and the utricles in your ears will be able to sense the vertical.

Pay attention to clues. Bubbles rise. A little water in your face mask will act like a carpenter's level. Your weights pull toward the bottom, while the air in your BC pulls toward the surface. If you can see your depth gauge, you will know whether you are going up. Water gets darker and colder as you descend. Going up, it will usually get brighter and warmer.

Rescue of others

If your buddy is acting strangely and his eyeballs are oscillating rapidly, or he is gyrating off in the wrong direction, stop him. Hold him tightly, look him sternly in the eye and signal him to go up with you. Make sure he is not holding his breath as you rise. Signal him to breathe if necessary. If there is an anchor line or ascent line handy, have him hold it to aid re-orientation.

Ear window rupture

A particularly serious underwater accident is to break one of the ear's two windows. These are thin, fibrous tissues covering two openings in the bony wall that separates the inner and the middle ear. An oval one receives sound vibrations from the three tiny bones that connect it to the eardrum. A round one, lower down, bulges out when the oval window bulges in, thus allowing equalization of high amplitude sound waves in the fluid of the inner ear.

Ear squeeze, regular or reverse, can rupture a window, but such an accident is more likely to happen during an over-zealous Valsalva maneuver (holding the nose and blowing to clear ears). Not only dizziness, but persistent ringing in the ear and a total loss of hearing can result. Surgical repair by an ear specialist is necessary.

To avoid rupturing a window, damaging an eardrum, or any of the other problems that can result from a forceful Valsalva maneuver (it can even cause heart irregularities), apply this Valsalva procedure slowly and cautiously.

Better yet, clear your ears via the Frenzel method. It is gentler. Instead of having your large chest muscles and diaphragm push air into the middle ear, you use the smaller force of your tongue. Hold your nose as in the Valsalva, then close off your larynx (as you do just before coughing), tense your mouth and throat muscles, and drive your tongue upward and backward. It is similar to swallowing. You will feel your eardrums bulge outward.

Fig. 9-8

Take a disorientated diver up on a line if possible.

Summary

With most physiological problems, the divers must surface

Some physiological problems render the diver vulnerable to varying degrees of disorientation or dislocation. Some of these can be overcome relatively easily, like cramps. More typically, however, physiological problems result in life-threatening emergencies which cannot be satisfactorily resolved underwater.

Almost always, a threat to respiratory or circulatory integrity will demand that the victim ascend as soon as possible. Ironically, in scuba diving, the move to safety itself can be inherently dangerous, compounding, rather than relieving the threat to life that necessitated the move in the first place.

As a result, life saving procedures depend on informed judgments about the best course of action from among unattractive alternatives.

CHAPTER 10

Diver to diver rescue

Your prevention measures did not work. A fellow diver is in trouble on the surface. You have to become involved.

Assess the situation

First, consider the best way to help. If no small boat, float or line can be used, a swimming rescue may be necessary. Call for help so others will follow or back you up. Swim head high to keep your eyes on the victim. If waves intervene, dry divers may point the way.

Constantly assess the condition of the victim, yourself and the environment and alter your approach if necessary. Keep the gear you are wearing if it will aid in the rescue. But do not hesitate to drop your tank or weight belt if you are certain they will hinder you and not be needed later.

Pace yourself to avoid exhaustion prior to completing the rescue. Use arm strokes as well as leg kicks.

Note the victim's approximate distance and direction so that, if he sinks while you are en route, you can get to the right spot, look for bubbles and follow them down. (Failing to find bubbles, check with the dry divers; if they have been alert, they will direct you to the location where the victim sank.)

If the victim is on the surface and conscious, shout to him and offer encouragement.

When a short distance away, a reassessment is in order. Is the victim breathing? Is he responsive? Can he help himself? Is contact necessary? Can you talk him out of his trouble? Is he panicky? How can you avoid endangering yourself? What is his gear configuration? How can you best use your equipment and his to aid the rescue? Many questions, but little time. An immediate decision is necessary. This reassessment should take only a second.

Restore easy breathing

In most cases, the rescuer's primary job is to restore easy breathing. This may be done by making air available, not only by using rescue breathing at the surface, or an auxiliary source underwater, but also by reducing exertion, providing physical support or buoyancy (floats, BCs, inflatable suits) and by reducing or submerging weights.

Equipment considerations

You should not *always* drop weights, inflate buoyancy devices, remove masks and jettison tanks. These actions help in many cases and cause problems in others.

Weights

Advantages of dropping weights

1. Buoyancy is increased. On the surface you will be able to float with your face above

Fig. 10-1

Do not drop weights when you have obstructions overhead.

water and breathe easily, assuming you are wearing a wet suit. If you ditch your weights on the bottom, the resulting buoyancy will usually (but not always) be enough to take you to the surface at a safe speed. You may have to kick to get started.

2. Towing a victim is easier if he has no weight belt because he assumes a more horizontal position in the water thereby reducing drag. Further, moving the mass of a heavy belt takes more energy even with plenty of buoyancy.

3. Removing a victim from the water will be considerably easier without weights.

Disadvantages of dropping weights

1. Once weights are gone, you lose the option of reversing your action.

2. Too many divers overweight themselves and depend on inflating a BC to obtain neutral buoyancy. Dropping such a heavy belt at depth will give instant buoyancy. Expanding BC air, unless vented, could cause an uncontrolled ascent.

3. If you drop your weight system while under a canopy of kelp or inside a cave or wreck, you might pin yourself to the ceiling.

4. The buoyancy of a wet suit is reduced considerably at depths below about 15 m (50 ft.). If air has not been added to the BC to compensate for this loss, dropping the weight belt will not necessarily make the diver float toward the surface.

5. One of the most obvious reasons for the rescuer to retain his weight belt is that he may have to duck underwater, get behind the victim in order to release his weight belt, inflate his vest or go after him if he sinks. The rescuer may also have to dive for a second victim.

6. The buoyancy of wet suit pants could make the rescuer's legs pop to the surface. As a result, skilled swimming is difficult. With inflatable dry suits, floundering is very likely, not only due to the increased buoyancy of the neoprene-covered legs, but also because removing the belt around the waist may allow the air formerly trapped by it in the chest area to flow into the lower part of the suit.

Safety divers might consider wearing two belts, each with half the usual weight so they can drop one and still handle a surface victim easily with adequate buoyancy. Some weights are made in two pieces and can be removed without unfastening the belt.

In summary, rescuers should drop the victim's weights in many cases...you will be there to keep the victim face-up. Retain the weights if there is an obstruction overhead, or if there is a problem that ditching weights would not solve. Retain your weights in almost all cases to handle a victim efficiently. Drop them if your safety or the rescue of a victim requires additional buoyancy or less mass.

Buoyancy devices

The rescuer must determine if and when to inflate his own BC and that of a victim. The advantages and disadvantages of such buoyancy must be considered prior to making the decision.

Advantages of inflating buoyancy compensators

1. In a surface emergency, obviously, an inflated buoyancy compensator will help keep your face above water. Underwater, it will bring you to the surface. (A few qualifications will be mentioned later.) If a BC has most of its air high in the chest area, it will turn you face-up on the surface even if you start face-down, limp and unconscious, neoprene suited and without weights.

2. Inflating a BC is a reversible action. You can deflate it slowly through the inflator hose or rapidly through the dump valve.

3. An inflated BC will make a diver more visible to potential helpers, especially when there are big waves.

Disadvantages of BC inflation The few advantages may completely offset the following disadvantages, most of which can be minimized:

1. A fully inflated BC may make breathing difficult if the straps are too tight. Equip-

ment will be harder to remove if buckles and straps are buried under a turgid BC. Let some air out. When suiting up, adjust the straps for a snug fit while the vest is fully inflated. If the straps are too loose, the BC may float up but leave you submerged. Or, it may ride up under your chin and tend to choke you, especially if you have no crotch strap and are loaded down with a heavy weight belt.

2. The larger and more inflated a BC, the more it will slow down a swimming diver, especially against a current. Inflate a BC only enough to achieve the buoyancy required.

3. An inflated BC may cause an uncontrolled ascent if the diver does not vent it sufficiently.

4. As a rescuer, you may want plenty of buoyancy when approaching a victim on the surface. However, if your BC has a small bore inflator hose and no dump valve, rapid deflation will be impossible. This becomes a problem if you must submerge to go after a sinking victim, to release his weight belt, or to inflate his vest.

5. During mouth-to-mouth resuscitation in open water, flotation helps. But with both of your BCs inflated—sometimes with only one inflated—you may have trouble getting close enough to the victim. Let out some air or use mouth-to-snorkel.

With backpack flotation BCs, mouth-to-mouth resuscitation may be difficult if either the rescuer's unit or the victim's unit is fully inflated. The air bladders get in the way. Deflating them partially may result in insufficient buoyancy due to the excessive weight usually carried with these systems. Consider mouth-to-snorkel. Some backpack BC units have quick releases that free the tank from the backpack. This allows the rescuer to retain the flotation while jettisoning the tank. However, check the backpacks you will be working with to be certain that the release opens wide enough for the tank to fall free without hanging up on the regulator attachments. Obviously, an inflator and other hoses must be pulled away from the BC first.

Fig. 10-2

Unless you know the "quick release" on the rig allows the tank to drop without snagging, do not attempt to detach the tank from the backpack.

Pros and cons of mask removal

1. Removing a mask is an irreversible action if you throw it away. In most cases, it is wise to save your own mask. If you must remove it, slip it over your arm or pull it down to one side of your neck.

2. Underwater, a mask is obviously desirable for clear vision and for keeping water out of the nose and eyes. On the surface, forward vision may be restricted by water drops or fog. Side vision may be restricted by the mask skirt. But if the mask is clear of water, it will still protect your eyes and nose.

3. If you want to improve your buoyancy by putting your face in the water and breathing through your snorkel, you will be more comfortable doing so with a mask.

4. On the surface, a rescuer will not normally want to remove his own mask. He should do so only after deciding that unrestricted vision is more important to him than protection from the water. (Of course, removing your mask *could* make your vision worse. Many divers have prescription lenses sealed to the face plate, if you lose such a mask, you may not even be able to see the boat!)

5. Removing the victim's mask allows you to see his face more clearly. His reaction to you, his facial expressions, his breathing (or lack of it) and his color will indicate his status. For these reasons it will usually be best to remove the mask of an unconscious victim on the surface.

6. A victim wearing a mask is protected from waves and spray. Water slapping his face, salt water in his eyes and up his nose may push a victim into panic. Therefore, during rough water conditions it is probably best to leave a conscious victim's mask on.

If the victim is claustrophobic and panicky, he may resolve the question for you by tearing off his mask as soon as he surfaces.

7. You may have to remove your own mask as well as the victim's for mouth-to-mouth resuscitation. If so, ditch the victim's mask, but save your own. Pull it down to the back of your neck or hook your arm through the strap. When you tire giving air mouth-to-mouth, you may switch to mouth-to-snorkel, using the snorkel attached to your mask.

In rough water, leave a conscious victim's mask on.

You may be able to give artificial respiration without removing either mask. Practice with your buddy. The victim's mask may seal his nose enough during mouth-to-mouth to free your hand for swimming support. The victim's snorkel will probably be positioned ready for mouth-to-snorkel resuscitation. His nose can be sealed by pinching through the mask or pushing up on its skirt.

8. You may need your mask to look for the victim's buddy underwater.

9. When rescuing an unconscious victim underwater, check his mask. If any water is inside, take the mask off as you start up with him. If it is only partially flooded, the expanding air as you rise could force water into his nose, triggering a laryngeal spasm. If his mask is full of water, it will have to be removed before the victim is given air. It will save time to remove it on the way up. If the mask is clear, leave it on. It will keep water from entering his nose.

Pros and cons of tank removal

1. Towing a victim's heavy, bulky tank takes energy and his dangling octopus and SPG hoses may impede your kick. You could tuck them out of the way. But his tank will probably have to be removed before lifting him from the water. Maybe the tank should be ditched before towing.

2. Tests have shown that a diver on the surface, experienced in tank removal can save time by removing his own tank whenever he must tow a victim on the surface 33 m (35 yds) or more.[1]

3. Jettisoning your tank is an irreversible procedure. You will not have it for resubmerging if you need to go after a second victim. However, if there is no other victim, if the tank is hindering your rescue or your safety and if you can remove it easily without jeopardizing the victim or yourself, you should probably ditch it.

4. If you decide to drop a tank, be sure to disconnect the automatic BC inflation hose. (Inflate the BC with it first if you need buoyancy.) Also, free any other hoses that may be tucked under a strap or into a pocket of the BC.

5. Safety divers, although suited-up and ready to enter the water at a moment's notice, frequently do not wear tanks. They reason that the rescues they have to make

[1]*Tests conducted during Project SLAM (Scuba Lifesaving & Accident Management), YMCA Center for Underwater ACtivities, Key West, Florida, November, 1977.*

will usually occur on the surface, and that a tank and regulator will slow them down. The wise safety diver, however, is ready when required to don a full tank with backpack and regulator attached, straps adjusted to fit.

6. Some tanks that are combined as a unit with a BC may be removed quickly to push, fully inflated, to support a victim, and/or to allow a rescuer freedom to handle a victim unencumbered.

7. The status of the victim's gear may indicate why he originally got into trouble. If you can do so without jeopardizing the safety of the victim, yourself or others, try to retain his gear or recover it after the rescue for future examination. Knowing the facts of accidents may save others from suffering similarly.

Surface rescues

You are more likely to have to rescue a diver on the surface than underwater. Remember, there are three kinds of victims: rational, panicky and passive or unconscious. Most of the problems of either the rational or the panicky victim can be solved by merely providing buoyant support.

Rational victim

You can help a rational surface victim fairly easily even if you do not have a float. However, before moving in be sure that he *is* rational and that he will probably stay that way. As long as he remains calm, you can work in close contact.

A continual assessment of the victim's condition is necessary. Determine his state of mind by communication and eye contact. Ask him what his problem is. You can tell his degree of stress by his responses. Reassure him.

Enlist the victim's cooperation. Get him to help himself. Involve him in establishing his own buoyancy. Get him to inflate his buoyancy compensator. Ask him to hand you anything he is carrying including, if he feels competent to do so, his weight belt. Do not jeopardize *your* safety; ditch them. If he still

is not buoyant, get him to neutralize the weight of his head by floating on his back or face-down, breathing through his snorkel.

If the victim is unable to do any of these things, you will have to make contact. Through your words and actions, the stricken diver should gain the impression that you are in complete control of the situation. If he realizes you know what you are doing, he will be more likely to cooperate.

Approach a rational victim cautiously and on his left side. (You will be closer to his BC inflator hose and actuator which are usually on the left.) You can support him quickly by placing a hand under his armpit or by holding a gear strap. You will be able to reach around to inflate his vest or drop his belt.

If making the victim buoyant and getting him to breathe easily does not solve his problem, you may have to help him to safety.

Panicky victim

If you have any doubt about your ability to handle a panic-stricken diver without endangering your own safety, do not get close. Call for help—preferably somebody with a float and line from the boat or shore—and wait for it. Meanwhile attempt to communicate with the victim. Shout if necessary to be sure he hears you over wind and waves. Try to get him to inflate his BC, drop his weights or lie on his back.

Sometimes a panicky victim can tell you what is wrong. You can gauge the degree of his stress by his tone of voice. It may be possible to calm him verbally and coax him to safety.

Watch the victim constantly, always assessing his status. Be prepared to get to him quickly if he goes unconscious. If he is non-buoyant, struggling with his head and shoulders above water, and then "calms down" by blacking out, he will submerge quickly, so you will have to go after him fast.

If the victim is still panicky on the surface, and no help is forthcoming, you might be able to remove your BC (assuming you are buoyant enough without it), inflate it and extend it to him. Holding a strap, tell him to

Fig. 10-4

Any sharp object in the hands of a panicky victim could rip your BC.

seize the BC without climbing on top of it. The buoyancy should calm him. You are now set to tow him. If the victim is still panicked and attempts to grab you, release the strap.

If you prefer not to remove your BC, if help is still not available, and if you think you can handle the victim safely, consider approaching him alone. But do not contact him until you have evaluated several key variables: the environment, your relative sizes, strengths, and degrees of fatigue, the gear available, his degree of panic, your training, experience, and state of mind.

Be extremely cautious. Your gear offers numerous hand holds that will help him climb on top of you. If he gets high enough, he could sink you. Any sharp object he may be carrying—a knife, a spear gun, a shell, a bit of salvage, a piece of coral—could rip your BC and eliminate your buoyancy. His frantic gyrations may knock away your mask, your regulator, or your fins.

All of these possibilities will be minimized if you approach from the rear. Stop talking to the victim and start breathing through your regulator: you will need the air if he sinks you. Try to swim around him. Once you are at his back, inflate your BC before contacting him.

As you swim he may turn to keep facing you. If you dive beneath him or submerge and swim around him, he is not likely to know where you are. Then you can surface behind him and make your initial contact. To submerge, you need to dump any air in your BC. (You have wisely retained your weight belt.) As you surface behind him, inflate your vest.

The least recommended system is an underwater approach. In this case, the rescuer submerges well out of the victim's reach but close enough to see him underwater. Swim to a point with your eyes nearly level with the victim's knees. Reverse your position, getting your fins under you. In the event the victim kicks, use one hand to protect you from his kicking and the other to reach up, inflate his BC and/or drop his weight belt. The resulting buoyancy may calm the victim, but do not depend on it. Turn him around, pulling one knee and pushing the other so his back will be toward you. Surface behind the victim holding his tank valve or gear straps so he will not be able to turn around.

Submerging to handle the victim may not be feasible in kelp beds, in surf or in low visibility water. Under such conditions, you may use a variation of the block and turn. After inflating your BC, grasp the victim's elbow (right to left or left to right) and turn him away

Fig. 10-5

Grasp victim's arm and turn him away from you so you'll be at his back.

from you. Again, control him using gear straps or tank valve so he is unable to turn back toward you.

You are now on the surface with the victim facing away from you. If you have not already done so, inflate the victim's BC, and drop his weight belt, then inflate your BC. To keep him from turning while you do all this, hold his tank between your knees.

If his inflator mechanism does not work, or if you do not want his BC fully inflated, you can pull his oral inflator hose around and blow it up by mouth. If his BC is over-inflated and it restricts his breathing, you can now let some air out.

If necessary, increase the victim's buoyancy by pushing the tank to a horizontal position so his head rests in the water. He is now at a good angle for towing.

If the victim is still panicky, do not attempt to remove his tank (or yours). You could easily lose control of him in the process.

Assistants can control the victim, remove gear and help you tow.

Defenses and escapes A diving victim is not likely to cause a rescuer as much trouble as the ordinary non-swimmer would in a near-drowning situation. A diver who is out

of his mind with panic however, presents a potentially lethal threat. He is unconcerned for your safety and is likely to climb onto you for air. The weight of his body and gear can sink you easily even if your BC is fully inflated.

If you fin hard to stay on the surface, you will simply encourage him to stay on top of you.

You may think, because you know lifesaving, you can release his hold and get away. Do not depend on it. Your tank valve, your hoses, your straps, and your hair are excellent hand-holds, almost impossible to break. And do not think you can cause a drowning victim enough pain to make him let go. Someone fighting for his life is not concerned about pain. The best answer is prevention. Stay out of the victim's reach. Face him or get behind him. Do not let him get behind you.

If he starts to grab for you, do whatever is necessary to avoid his clutches. Duck, dodge, pivot, block, parry, push him away or turn him. Use your arms and knees: because flippers drag in the water, you probably will not be able to bring your feet up fast enough.

If you do get caught, you will probably go under as the victim climbs on you for air. Your first consideration is insuring your own air supply. If you have no regulator in your

Fig. 10-6

If caught, suck *in air,* tuck *your chin, and* duck *under the water.*

mouth, try to get a bite of air before going under. Tuck your chin to avoid the sort of pressure that can collapse your windpipe or carotid arteries. If you submerge yourself as he grabs, he will probably let go. He might not. Divers have been known to retain a strong grip even after blacking out.

If you were using your regulator before the grab, and the victim has not knocked it away, you should be able to breathe after he has forced you under. You can now take your time activating *his* BC inflator or dropping his weights. Once buoyant, he will probably let go. Do not inflate your own BC before making the victim buoyant. You will only make yourself a more desirable object to clutch for support.

Fig. 10-7

If you have air, you have time. Make victim buoyant.

Keep track of your buddy on the surface.

If you are caught without a regulator in your mouth, you may be able to insert your regulator and breathe. If not, you still may be able to pop his vest or drop his weight belt. This will not be easy if he has knocked away your mask or is holding you tightly. Practice without a mask and see.

If you cannot activate his BC or drop his weights, you still may be able to escape. To escape from either a front or a rear head hold, push up sharply on the victim's elbows with both hands as you duck your head and tuck your chin. Then quickly swim down and away from his reach. You will probably lose your mask and regulator in the process. You can retrieve your regulator later, but your mask may be gone.

If the victim grabs one of your wrists with both hands, work against his thumbs. Reach through his arms to grab your own hand. Then forcefully pull it away, up and toward you. Move away fast.

You could be caught unexpectedly by a victim you were not trying to rescue. Therefore, even if you doubt that you would ever try to save someone, you should practice these techniques. It might be *your* life you save. During practice, both victim and rescuer should know the signal to release a hold. Two taps to the body is standard. If it is ignored, two pinches can be used.

Unconscious or passive victim

Any diver who remains motionless on the surface for a substantial period of time should be checked. He might be unconscious, semiconscious, frozen with fear or on the verge of blacking out from exhaustion or hypothermia. Approach with caution.

Case studies at the National Underwater Accident Data Center reveal that "Much more common than the active drowning victim is a partial loss of consciousness or ability to deal with the situation. Most typically the victim lags behind, seems confused or vague and then suddenly slips underwater, often to be lost for a considerable period of time....It is the passivity of the victim, his total inability to look after himself, and his apparent willingness to sink below the surface that appears again and again in case narratives by buddy divers and other witnesses."[2]

As soon as you identify a passive victim, call for help. Quick action is necessary. A non-

[2]*Hilbert V. Schenck & John McAniff*, U.S. Underwater Fatality Statistics - 1973, U. of Rhode Island, Report No. URI-SSR-75-9, May, 1975, page 36.

Fig. 10-9

Consider giving an unconscious victim your regulator to keep him from inhaling water.

buoyant victim who has just lapsed into unconsciousness will silently sink. If an unconscious victim is slightly buoyant but stops breathing, the water pressure on the chest may force him to exhale. He will lose buoyancy and go under.

Regardless of his position, determine that a victim is breathing and prevent him from sinking.

Breaths can be hard to detect. You may see the victim's nose and lips move slightly. You may also see the mist of his exhalations if the air is cold.

If the victim is cyanotic, you can be certain he needs air. Give him four quick but full breaths immediately and continue regular rescue breathing. If you are unable to determine if he is breathing, assume he is not and give him air. If you detect any feeble attempts at respiration, synchronize your breaths with his. Between breaths, make yourself and the victim buoyant enough for efficient artificial respiration.

When a passive victim is stabilized, buoyant, and breathing easily, watch carefully to be sure breathing continues.

If either your regulator or his has adequate air, consider giving it to him so waves will not slop into his mouth. (You will probably have to hold the regulator in his mouth.)

Underwater rescues

Life saving rarely occurs underwater. A main reason is a failure to keep track of fellow divers. To make a rescue you must be close enough to help, observant enough to notice a problem and skilled enough to solve it.

Rational victim

A rational diver seen in trouble underwater usually presents few problems unless he becomes panicky. Continually assess his condition. After making certain the victim has adequate air, communicate how you will help. Unless the trouble keeps you from ascending, surface together and discuss the problem. If it can be solved, go back down. If not, abort the dive.

Panicky victim

A panicky victim underwater is dangerous. As a rescuer, you are vulnerable to loss of air supply, loss of gear, entanglement, and unexpected BC inflation (or deflation). You are also vulnerable to overexertion. Whenever you struggle with an irrational diver underwater, the stress may seriously reduce your effectiveness and may even cause *you* to panic. Also, you risk overbreathing your regulator—especially at depth. In addition, many regulators are less efficient when the tank pressure is down. Remember, when a

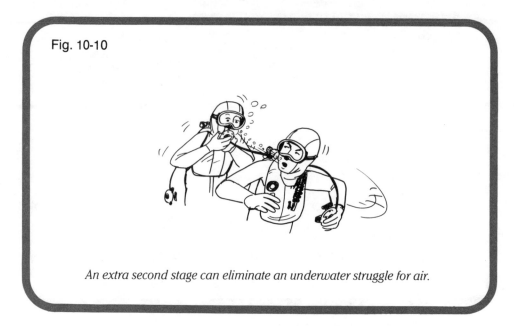

Fig. 10-10

An extra second stage can eliminate an underwater struggle for air.

buddy's tank is dry, your own supply is probably so low that you may be lucky to get enough air even if your gear remains intact. So avoid an underwater struggle.

Panic underwater is most frequently caused either by an actual loss of air or by the fear of losing it. The victim may think he is out of air when he is not. A more usual problem is the kind of erratic breathing that creates feelings of air hunger.

Without getting dangerously close, you *may* be able to help this victim by signaling him to stop, take it easy, slow down, and exhale. Unfortunately, it is unlikely that a frantic diver will even notice your signals. If you signal him to ascend, however, and then start up, he may follow you.

It is possible that your breathless buddy, in his unreasoning state, has forgotten what kind of gear he is wearing. You may notice a "J" valve reserve in the up position. If so, push it down to give him instant relief. Getting that close, however, will expose you to danger unless you approach him from the rear.

If you have been monitoring your buddy's tank reserves as well as your own, neither of you is likely to run out of air unexpectedly. But if your vigilance lapses, you may sud-

denly find that your regulator has been snatched from your mouth. You will be glad then if you have a spare second stage (octopus) or auxiliary air system (pony bottle or extra tank).

In the absence of these systems, you still have alternatives. If your buoyancy compensator uses a tank inflator and if you have practiced BC breathing, you can let the panicked diver keep your regulator while you breathe from your BC and surface with him.

Trying to buddy-breathe with a panicky victim is dangerous. Buddy breathing requires the kind of cooperation that an irrational diver is unlikely to give. If you give him your regulator, do not expect to get it back.

If the victim's panic was caused by strangling on water in his airways, he probably will not try to get air from anyone underwater. He will head for the surface, holding his breath, risking a lung rupture. Trying to stop such a victim could be dangerous. In the excitement you are liable to hold *your* breath as he drags you up. Thus, if you do try to stop him, remember to keep breathing. You may not be able to grab anything but his fins, but this will slow his propulsion even if they come off in your hands. Upon stopping the victim, get a strong grip on him, look him sternly in the eye, and signal him to exhale.

Fig. 10-11

You may slow the panicked ascent of a non-breathing diver by seizing his fins.

In cases of extreme fear, victims cannot be successfully forced to exhale. Do not punch him in the chest. This may cause either the air embolism you are trying to avoid, or other problems.

One final caution: Do not attempt to stop a "victim" who is exhaling freely as he rises. You might interrupt a planned emergency ascent by a fully rational diver, thereby multiplying his problems.

Unconscious breathing victim

A motionless diver on the bottom could be unconscious. If groups of bubbles rise intermittently he is obviously breathing, but this does not mean he has not blacked out. A slumped position, extremities at grotesque angles, face buried in the sand, eyes closed, or staring at nothing—all could indicate unconsciousness. Check to make sure.

If you get no reaction, or a feeble one, your job is to keep the victim breathing (without his inhaling water) and get him to the surface swiftly. Approach from the rear or side. Extend one arm and encircle the victim's head tightly against your chest.

To keep him breathing, hold his regulator in his mouth—carefully, to avoid blocking air flow—and tilt his head back to keep his airway open.

Water could enter the airway through his nose. Check his mask. If it is clear, leave it on. If there is any water inside, remove the mask. With his mask off, seal his nose without dislodging the regulator.

Because he has air in his lungs, the victim is probably close to neutral buoyancy. Start up with him at the normal 18 m (60 ft.)/minute. If you need more buoyancy, drop his weights or inflate his BC. You have a free hand to do this.

Unconscious non-breathing victim

A motionless diver underwater who is not cycling bubbles is obviously not breathing. Although lung rupture, decompression sickness, and inhalation of water are risks worth worrying about, the victim's primary need is air.

The surface is the most logical source of air. However, as a deeply anoxic victim ascends through shallow water, the partial pressure of oxygen in his lungs, already extremely low, will be reduced even more. The resulting rapid reduction of oxygen in the blood supply to the victim's vital brain tissues could quickly cause his death. Dr. George Harpur states that, to minimize this effect, and to save the victim's life, he must be sent through this shallow water zone as quickly as possible, even if the rescuer cannot safely keep pace. Dr. Harpur suggests that, after raising the victim from a horizontal position on the bottom to the vertical, he be made fully buoyant and "allowed to ascend, the rescuer following at a safe rate, to institute artificial respiration on the surface."[3]

When the victim arrives at the surface, he will first shoot from the water, then fall back into a horizontal position supported by his BC, which (if standard) will float him on his back. The sudden removal of water pressure from his chest may result in a passive inhalation of 600 to 900 cm^2 of air.

Harpur indicates that experiments have shown that an *unconscious* victim will probably tolerate very rapid ascents without lung rupture, even with the head slumped forward. Air escapes from the chest easily owing to a one-way valve effect. Thus, air embolism is not a usual danger for an *unconscious* victim.[3]

Some divers have serious misgivings about letting an unconscious victim go up uncontrolled. This "send him up" technique is obviously not recommended if the surface is obstructed. There may be other problems. Getting the victim very buoyant is not always possible, especially at depth. His wet suit will be compressed, reducing its buoyancy. Dropping his weights may make very little difference.

The victim must have the right kind of buoyancy device. Unless the water is very shallow, or the CO_2 cartridge is extra large, inflating the cartridge will not necessarily speed the victim to the surface. It may not expand the vest fully. If a CO_2 vest has air inside from prior use as a buoyancy compensator, and has no overpressure valve, expansion of the gas as it approaches the surface could rupture the vest and make it useless. Also, the buoyancy device must be one that will float the victim face up on the surface while awaiting the rescuer. If it is dark, if waves are high, or if there is a strong current, finding the victim on the surface will be difficult.

However, if none of these problems is present, and if you are close to the no-decompression limits (or need to decompress on the way up) so that you would endanger yourself by a rapid ascent, sending the victim up on a fast buoyant ascent is probably the best way to save him.

The most universally accepted method of rescuing an unconscious, non-breathing victim underwater is to grab him and go, wasting no time on the bottom. When you start to lift him, expect him to be heavy. Removing his weight belt is almost invariably essential.

You may have to inflate his buoyancy device, and possibly your own to get him off the bottom.

Do not waste time on the bottom. If the surface is close, don't worry about *how* you get the victim up. (Remember to keep *your* airway open.) However, if the water is deep, surfacing will take time. On the way up, without slowing your ascent, you *may* be able to do a few things that will make the rescue safer for both you and the victim.

If you are ascending too fast due to excessive buoyancy, control your speed by venting air from a BC. If the victim's regulator is in his mouth when you find him, hold it there. An unconscious victim can vent air freely with his head flopped forward, but air going in may be blocked. Therefore, if his regulator is in place, tilt his head back to keep his airway open. If he gasps, he'll get no water, but may be *some* air.

If the victim's regulator is not in place when you find him, leave it out and don't tilt his head back. Hyperextending the neck might let water in his mouth trickle into his windpipe, even if air is flowing out. A laryngospasm could result.

In summary, if the victim's regulator is in his mouth, hold it in and tilt his head back. If the regulator is out, leave it out and don't tilt the head back. If the victim's mask is on and clear, leave it on. If there is water inside, remove the mask. If you are tilting a maskless victim's head back, pinch his nose.

Should you press the victim's chest or abdomen during ascent to make him exhale? Most authorities agree that this isn't neces-

[3]*George Harpur, M.D., "Ninety Seconds Deep Scuba Rescue," NAUI News, January, 1974, pages 4-8.*

Fig. 10-12

An unconscious, non-breathing victim will be heavy. His lungs will have very little air and may be full of water.

sary. An unconscious victim is not trying to hold his breath, and air will escape passively.

The victim could revive and panic. Unconsciousness produced by lack of oxygen to the brain typically involves a temporary memory loss. The victim may not even remember that he was diving, and when he awakens to find himself being towed underwater, he nat-

urally experiences great fear. So be on guard. If the victim panics, you will have to protect yourself while keeping his mask and regulator in place. Use both of your hands. If you are behind him, and holding his head tightly, there is not much he can do to you. However, if he is endangering your safety, do not hesitate to let him go and save yourself.

Fig. 10-13

Ascending from the depths with the victim's mask on or off.

None of these operations—mask checking and removal, regulator snugging, head extension, nose pinching—should be undertaken if it will delay your ascent. You can easily become so involved in handling the victim that you forget to ascend immediately and continuously. Keep in mind that the victim's primary need is air and that there is plenty of air at the surface. If the surface is close you will not have time to do anything while ascending.

Summary

Diver rescue

- Scuba divers have an advantage over non-scuba rescuers in that both the rescuer and victim have a readily available buoyant support.
- Equipment can be a distinct disadvantage in many emergencies; sometimes because it makes a rescue more complex.
- The decision to remove and/or ditch equipment, when and how, is not as straightforward as it might appear.
- The choice of life saving procedure will depend upon many factors.
- Victim types:
  conscious or unconscious
  breathing or non-breathing
  injured or uninjured
  combinations of these
- All conscious victims will display signs of varying degrees of stress.
- The rescuer must be aware of the likely behavior patterns of both rational and panicked victims.
- The rescuer should be especially alert for signs of change in the victim's behavior in order to take the appropriate defensive action.

Open water resuscitation

11

An unconscious nonbreathing victim on the surface needs air fast. There are two ways to deliver this vital air—mouth-to-mouth (or nose) and mouth-to-snorkel. Mouth-to-mouth is uncomplicated, but without flotation or fins it is also very tiring. In contrast, you will not get as tired giving air mouth-to-snorkel because you do not have to lift your head above water. It requires practice to make a good seal over the victim's lips with the snorkel mouthpiece.

Mouth-to-mouth

Without fins or flotation, you can give a *few* breaths of air to a non-breathing victim if you are a strong swimmer and can tread water efficiently. These are the steps in the procedure:

1. As you approach the victim, pull your mask down to your neck or pull it over your arm. Get the victim's face above water with a chin pull. As you check for breathing, pull down the corner of his mouth and allow any water to drain out.

Do not delay in this or any other preliminary. Take only a second.

2. Hook your free arm over the victim's near arm and place the back of your hand against the back of his neck, forming a fulcrum to tilt his head. (It may be easier for you not to interlock arms, especially if you are much smaller than the victim. If so, simply cradle the victim's neck with your free hand without placing your arm over his arm.) If the victim is wearing a back-mounted BC, instead of locking arms, grasp the shoulder strap of the backpack. If you can, support the victim's neck between your thumb and forefinger. Alternately you could hold the victim's hair or hood. If scuba gear interferes, use any convenient spot for your hand near the back of his neck.

3. Release the chin pull, and press the heel of that hand on the victim's forehead, tilting his head back for an open airway. Now you can easily pinch his nostrils with your thumb and forefinger.

4. Turn his head and body toward you. Seal your mouth over his and give four full, quick breaths followed by normal rescue breathing. Do not waste time dropping weights or inflating BCs before attempting to give air. Handle gear afterwards, between breaths. If you fail to get air in on the first try, *then* make him buoyant. If you can make a lip seal with your mask on, do so. It will keep the water from your eyes and nose.

Fig. 11-1

Positioning for mouth-to-mouth.

The initial chin pull position (which precedes both mouth-to-mouth and mouth-to-snorkel methods) must firmly secure the victim's head in the crook of your arm, or against your chest. This affords complete control in order that the victim will not drift away in waves or current.

Travel head first with the victim while treading water. The forward momentum will help keep both of your faces out of the water. Also, the more parallel to the surface you can get, the less likely you are to be swamped by waves. Instead, the waves will buoy you up.

Fig. 11-2

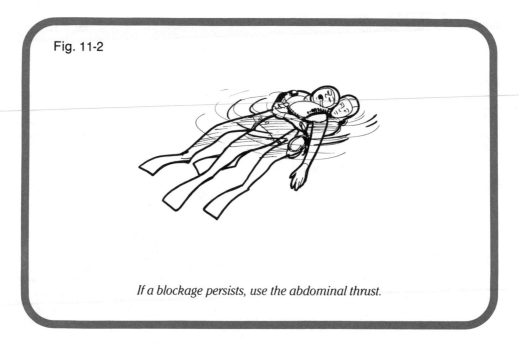

If a blockage persists, use the abdominal thrust.

Press your mouth tightly over the victim's lips, maintaining the seal while you blow. If you sense a blockage, tilt his head back further.

Be prepared for the victim to vomit. Clear the mouth by sweeping it out with your fingers.

By turning the victim's upper body towards you, it is possible to create a mouth-to-mouth seal while keeping your head relatively low in the water. If you do not turn his body, the weight of your head above the water may force his face—and yours—under before you can make a good seal. However, if the seal is water-tight before you go under, give the victim an immediate breath; you can successfully blow air into him even if both your faces are submerged. Of course, his face must be above the surface before you release your seal and allow him to exhale. Pause above the surface before breaking mouth contact to let water drain down past the victim's mouth.

Your fins allow you to get high enough to place your mouth over the victim's. The buoyancy of an inflated BC on the victim can prevent his sinking when you make mouth contact.

Do not inflate both buoyancy compensators. The extra bulk will probably keep you from getting close enough for mouth contact. Even one full BC may be too bulky. If so, release some air.

Dropping the victim's weight belt also adds buoyancy. But be sure to get some air into him first, in case you have to struggle with the belt. THE VICTIM'S PRIMARY NEED IS AIR. ATTEMPT TO REMOVE OR MANIPULATE GEAR ONLY AFTER GIVING FOUR QUICK, FULL BREATHS. If you need to swim to stay afloat, give air between arm strokes.

Try sealing the victim's nostrils by pressing your cheek up against his nose (or his mask, if left on), thus freeing an arm for swimming support. If you cannot seal his nose perfectly, do not worry. His mask may seal his nose well enough so you can use your arm to swim.

Pay attention to wave action. You may be able to avoid flooding the victim by holding him on his leeward side (away from the wind), turning his head away from the waves, and timing your breaths so that, when a wave breaks over you, your mouths are sealed. Do not worry about rhythm. Inflating the victim's lungs fully and frequently, without introducing water, is much more important than giving one breath in each 5

Fig. 11-3

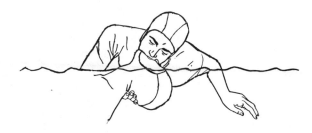

You may be able to free an arm for swimming support if you seal victim's nose with your cheek.

Fig. 11-4

Watch wave action and protect victim's airways from water.

second interval. If you see a swamping wave approaching, seal the victim's mouth and nose with your hand while it passes.

During practice, the victim can help you by relaxing all muscles, inhaling slightly and allowing you to blow into the lungs. Blow gently at first. If you create a strong gust, your practice victim may block the flow of air by closing his throat. A gentle pressure at first will encourage him to let his lungs fill.

When you are adept at mouth-to-mouth in shallow water, try it in deep water. It helps to wear fins or some kind of flotation. If you and your buddy try your BCs in practice, you will know whether one or both will be useful in a rescue.

When you are confident of your ability to give air mouth-to-mouth using flotation, try it without any added buoyancy. Practice also with the combinations of scuba or snorkling

Fig. 11-5

An extra rescuer can help support victim and be ready to give mouth-to-mouth when the original rescuer tires. Third rescuer can assist with gear and push victim towards safety.

gear you will be wearing in open water—wet suit, tank, weight belt, buoyancy compensator. Begin by wearing only wet suit gloves. They will make your hands feel clumsy at first. Continue practicing in open water under varied conditions of waves and current.

Backpack-mounted BCs that have their flotation bladders around the tank will make giving air mouth-to-mouth difficult if either the victim's unit or yours is fully inflated. The air bladders get in the way. Deflating them partially may result in insufficient buoyancy because divers who wear them are frequently overweighted. If you ditch the weights, extra energy may be needed to keep fully inflated bladders from floating you or the victim face down. Partial inflation, just sufficient for adequate buoyancy, will minimize both problems.

Mouth-to-snorkel

The tiring task of lifting your head high out of the water to seal your mouths can be eliminated by using a snorkel for rescue breathing.

1. Get the victim's face above water with a chin pull, and hold his head against your chest.

2. With your free hand, hold the snorkel above the surface and let the water run out (or blow it out). Keep it clear by aiming or bending the tube end up, or by holding it in your mouth. (You can breathe through the tube while lining up the mouthpiece over the victim's mouth.) You can bend most tubes by pressing on top with your middle and ring fingers as you push from underneath with your thumb and other fingers.

3. Release your fingers from the chin pull to receive the snorkel mouthpiece between your middle and ring fingers, maintaining control of the victim's head by holding his chin tightly between your wrist and your chest.

4. Place the snorkel flange over the victim's mouth. Your fingers should press tightly all the way around the snorkel flange. Watch what you are doing to be sure the snorkel mouthpiece is over his open lips.

5. Seal his nose with the thumb and forefinger or push the side of your forefinger against his nostrils. If the victim's mask is still on, you may close his nostrils by pressing against the mask at the nostrils depending upon the configuration of the mask.

6. Place the tube end of the snorkel in your

Fig. 11-6

To keep the snorkel dry after clearing, bend the tube end up.

Fig. 11-7

Hold the victim's head against your chest with your wrist as you insert the snorkel flange between your middle and ring fingers.

mouth with your other hand and blow. Give four quick, full breaths. To overcome the dead air space in the snorkel, blow slightly longer than you would for mouth-to-mouth.

7. After filling the victim's lungs, remove the tube end from your mouth and allow the air to escape from the tube. Listen for the sound of exhaled air or feel it on your cheek.

8. Continue rescue breathing as you tow the victim to safety. On your back with your head in the water, you are in a good position for towing.

Fig. 11-8

Test your seal by submerging your practice victim's face to simulate a wave washing over him.

If your mouthpiece seal is imperfect or if the victim's nostrils are not pinched shut, you may feel air escaping around your fingers, or will notice that chest pressure fails to build as you blow. Readjust your fingers to create a better seal. If you feel an air blockage, tilt his head back further. If you are still unable to get air into him, try abdominal thrusts.

As a rescuer, you may become dizzy from hyperventilation. If so, slow down.

An almost perfect seal results when the snorkel flange is inserted between the victim's lips and teeth. This is difficult to achieve on an unconscious victim. But if you can't make an adequate seal with the flange outside his lips, give four quick, full breaths, mouth-to-mouth. This will allow time to insert the flange between his lips and teeth.

Most snorkels will work, including contoured types and those with corrugated tubes, but some work better than others. You must be able to aim the mouthpiece down over the lips and still keep the tube end out of the water. So the tube must have a natural curve in the right direction, be flexible enough to bend, or the mouthpiece must bend or swivel. Check your snorkel and see how it works. A few are too rigid to be useful. Some,

if bent too sharply will cut off air. If too long, it will be difficult to keep a good seal while blowing. You may wish to shorten yours. A wide flange makes a better seal over the outside of the lips, while a narrow flange is easier to get inside the mouth. And some snorkel designs leave very little room for your fingers to fit behind the flange.

Snorkels with purge valves will work if you block the valve with your fingers or palm. This requires two hands so hold the tube end between your teeth, letting the victim's exhalations flow away from your mouth as you inhale.

Holding the snorkel this way also allows using both hands to seal the mouthpiece more easily between the victim's lips and teeth. If there is no purge valve, it frees a hand for swimming support or manipulating gear.

If you must use a snorkel that is tightly attached to a mask, don't bother separating them. Just let the mask dangle. It will not be in the way. If a victim is wearing a mask, and you are sure it is clear of water, it may be left on. It will protect the face from waves and spray.

Fig. 11-9

Holding the snorkel tube between your teeth allows a free hand to seal a purge valve, make a better mouth seal, or for swimming support. Just don't inhale the victim's stale air.

If a victim vomits, you will have to remove the snorkel, clear his mouth, swish the snorkel through the water to clear it, let it drain, replace it, and start over.

Mouth-to-mouth vs mouth-to-snorkel

The sooner rescue breathing commences, the better. If you can perform mouth-to-mouth, by all means do so; however, it may be hard to sustain in deep water. Treading high enough to reach the victim's mouth and keeping his face above the surface for his exhalations may soon exhaust the rescuer, especially in rough water. Flotation helps, but the necessity of close contact prevents full inflation of both vests.

With mouth-to-snorkel a rescuer can give air successfully while his head stays low in the water. Since your heads need not be as close as with mouth-to-mouth, you can use the full flotation of both buoyancy compensators to ride higher above any chop. Even without such buoyancy, both of you will be more horizontal in the water, thus, offering less drag and allowing waves and swell to buoy you up instead of swamping you.

People may be less inhibited to practice mouth-to-snorkel. A well rehearsed mouth-to-snorkel rescue will naturally go better than a poorly rehearsed mouth-to-mouth rescue.

Mouth-to-snorkel has some obvious disadvantages. The snorkel must be adaptable to the technique; some are impossible to use. Compared with mouth-to-mouth, mouth-to-snorkel takes more time and manual dexterity (and practice) to create the seal. And it is not as easy to watch the victim's face or to detect vomiting. Finally, if the victim has dentures, they are more likely to dislodge and cause problems.

Which should you choose? Usually the specific circumstances of the accident dictate that one method be preferred over the other—or that both be used. Try mouth-to-mouth first if you can, to get a few quick, full breaths into the victim. Then switch to mouth-to-snorkel for the long haul. If you have practiced both, chances for a successful

rescue are doubled. The greater our repertoire of skills, the better.

Underwater resuscitation

Authorities agree that normally you should not attempt to give air to an unconscious, non-breathing victim on the bottom. You are liable to waste valuable air and time, endanger yourself, or inadvertently drown the victim, especially if he revives and panics while underwater. However, if the surface is simply not available, for example: in long distance penetration cave diving, wreck diving, under-ice diving, and saturation diving, you might be justified in attempting artificial respiration.

The methods are difficult and may make the situation worse unless you are well-trained, teamed with one or more other rescuers, and have spare regulators with plenty of air. If you are going to do penetration or saturation diving, you should learn about these possible techniques. You could save a life.

Providing air utilizing the purge valve

Forcing air into a victim by alternately pushing the purge valve has worked in an actual rescue. But there is a potential problem: you cannot guarantee that air will enter the victim's lungs when the purge button is pushed. It may all go out the exhalation ports and be wasted. If you attempt to obstruct this flow, the full pressure, up to 180 psi over ambient, could rupture the lungs. (Some regulators might over-pressure lungs even with both exhalation ports wide open. However, you would perhaps be justified in taking a chance with an unknown regulator to save a life.)

To avoid forcing water into the lungs, the regulator must be cleared.

If an unconscious victim's neck is flexed (chin touching his chest), his airway will probably be closed and block the flow of air into his lungs. With this in mind, you have a method of purging the water from the victim's regulator and his upper airways. After inserting a regulator, pinch the victim's nostrils shut, turn his face down, neck flexed, seal his lips around the mouthpiece flange, and push the purge button momentarily. Air should flow in and expand the victim's cheeks. When you release the button, ambient pressure will force the water out. No water, bubbles, or spray should reach the victim's lungs. It should be blocked so it will not get to his larynx avoiding a laryngeal spasm. Open the victim's airway by extending his neck, sealing his nostrils (and the mouthpiece), and push the purge button intermittently to deliver air.

Air flowing into his airways will not necessarily inflate the victim's lungs. If his chest does not expand and if the victim does not exhale air passively after you have released the purge button, he probably is not getting air. All air may go out the exhalation ports.

Manual method of resuscitation

Prior to the recognition of mouth-to-mouth's superior efficiency, various methods of compressing the chest were reported to have revived many non-breathing victims. If a purged regulator is held in the victim's mouth and if his head is extended and his nose sealed, you may ventilate him by encircling his chest and alternately squeezing and relaxing. The volume of air delivered by this method will not approach the levels achieved by mouth-to-mouth on land, but it may be enough to keep his heart going as you make your way to safety.

This technique is almost impossible for one rescuer. You only have one hand available for squeezing the victim's chest. The other is fully occupied sealing the regulator in the victim's mouth and pinching his nostrils while extending his head.

Because these techniques have limitations, what should you do when confronted with an unconscious, non-breathing victim while confined underwater? If the distance to safety is short, do not waste time trying to ventilate. Get the victim to the surface as fast as you can. But, if you have to travel so far that the victim could not possibly survive, if you are confident of your ability, if you have competent help so that you would not jeopardize your own safety or that of fellow rescuers, and if there is plenty of air available, trying to give the victim air while underwater may be worthwhile.

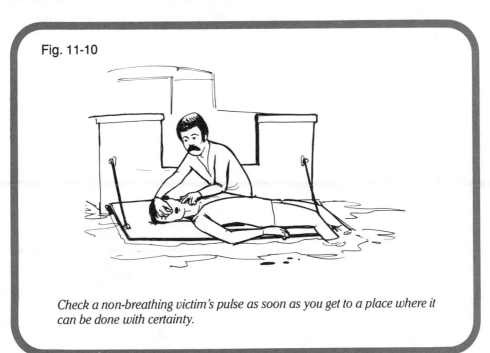

Fig. 11-10

Check a non-breathing victim's pulse as soon as you get to a place where it can be done with certainty.

Fig. 11-11

Two-rescuer CPR in open water.

Cardiac arrest in open water

A victim without air quickly becomes cyanotic. His lips and skin may turn blue or ashen gray. With his lungs ventilated, the victim's color should return to a livelier pink. If this does not happen soon after you have started rescue breathing, his heart may have stopped.

If you suspect that the victim's heart has stopped, be prepared to deal with this crisis the second he is in shallow water or at the side of a boat. Remove your gloves, unzip his wet suit jacket, fold back his hood, and check the carotid pulse. If there is no pulse, get the victim out of the water fast and onto a hard flat surface where conventional CPR can be given.

A number of methods have been suggested for CPR in open water. Most of them involve using specialized equipment, such as: paddleboards, harnesses, lines or especially finetuned scuba regulators. Without a firm surface support, perhaps the simplest method recommends one rescuer to use his fists to compress the victim's chest using his own chest as a back support. The second rescuer gives mouth-to-snorkel rescue breathing.

The main disadvantage of any open water CPR method is that it is extremely difficult to determine that a victim's heart has actually stopped breathing. Therefore, if the distance is short, do not waste time attempting to check a pulse or start CPR. Continue rescue breathing and get the victim to a boat or shore where effective CPR can be given. Full breaths alone may even re-start a heart that has not been stopped too long.[1]

However if the distance is great, and two experienced rescuers are available who have practiced the technique, and are certain the victim's heart has stopped, attempt open water CPR.

[1]*Dr. Christopher W. Dueker, M.D.*, Medical Aspects of Sport Diving, *page 192.*

Summary

Resuscitation in open water

MOUTH-TO-MOUTH. At the surface immediately check for breathing in the unconscious victim. Drain the mouth as you check, if the victim is not breathing, administer four quick breaths followed by normal rescue breathing.

Do not attempt to manipulate or remove gear until rescue breathing is established.

MOUTH-TO-SNORKEL. In some instances, and with an experienced rescuer, rescue breathing is administered by the rescuer blowing into the snorkel held in the victim's mouth. This technique may be useful in instances where the rescuer becomes quickly fatigued through treading high enough to administer effective mouth-to-mouth.

CARDIAC ARREST. Absence of a carotid pulse indicates the heart has stopped. Get the victim out of the water fast and onto a hard flat surface where CPR can be administered.

Note: Divers who are reluctant to learn and practice resuscitation skills are NOT suitable buddies on a dive.

Towing

12

Once you have the immediate emergency under control, prepare to tow the victim. Consider heading for the nearest safety: another boat, the shore, a sand bar, a rock, or a pier for instance. This location will be determined by the follow up care needed.

Solicit help from any conceivable source. It could come from a dive boat, a fishing boat or the shore. Whoever is available can help support the victim, tow, remove gear, observe conditions and alternate with you during resuscitation.

Talk to the victim. Encourage him to help

you. He may be able to remove his gear, inflate or deflate his BC, or help propel himself with arms or fins. However, if the victim is unable to help propel, tell him to keep his arms at his side and his head in the water to reduce drag and increase buoyancy.

This chapter discusses several ways to tow a victim. Practice many different tows so you can meet a variety of crises. What will you substitute for the tank-valve tow if the tank is ditched?

Consider the following discussion of towing principles and, in your rescue, select the tow

Fig. 12-1

It may be best to tow a victim away from his starting point to a closer spot more suitable for first aid.

that meets the specific demands of the accident and the environment.

Rescuer safety

- Never jeopardize your own safety.
- Know your limitations.
- Do not try to tow a panicky victim without a float or help. If you think the situation argues against rescue, wait for help instead—or change the situation.
- Ditch encumbrances or adjust buoyancy in order that you can handle the victim.
- Continually reassess your safety during the tow.
- Be prepared to protect yourself if the victim panics. Release him to save yourself if necessary.
- Position the victim between you and any rocks or pilings so that he will take the brunt of collisions. This sounds hardhearted, but if you become disabled and cannot continue the rescue, both of you may drown.

- Pace yourself to avoid exhaustion.
- Change your kick to use different muscle groups and relieve fatigue.

Victim safety

- A primary concern during a tow is that the victim continues breathing. Keep the airway clear. If he is conscious, keep his face above the surface. If he is not breathing administer rescue breathing.
- If the victim's mask is flooded, lift its skirt briefly and allow the water to drain. If waves are not a problem, remove the victim's mask for a clearer view of his face.
- If either your tank or the victim's has adequate air, holding the regulator in his mouth will simultaneously supply air and block water. If no regulator with air is available, you will have to watch the water and cover the victim's mouth (and nose, if he is not wearing a mask) with your hand whenever a wave breaks over you.
- Frequent eye contact reassures a conscious victim and gives you an indication of any changes in his condition. An unconscious victim must be monitored constantly to be sure he is breathing and not vomiting.
- A victim suffering from any serious injury

Fig. 12-2

On the surface, lift the mask skirt to drain water and replace it to protect victim's face from waves and spray.

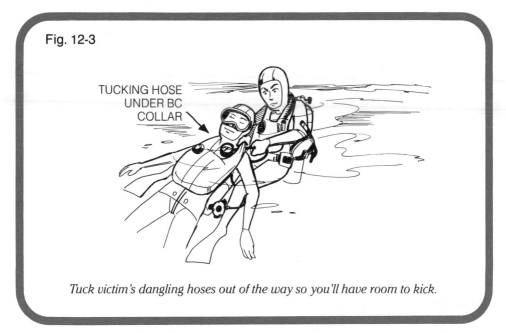

Fig. 12-3

TUCKING HOSE
UNDER BC
COLLAR

Tuck victim's dangling hoses out of the way so you'll have room to kick.

is also probably suffering from shock. Exercise could make the condition worse; do not allow him to swim. Tow him instead.

- A victim with a suspected spinal injury needs a special tow that keeps his head and body in a straight line.

Control of the victim

Do not assume that a cold, tired, weak or passive diver will hold on to you. He may let go and sink or drift away. Tight physical control of the victim is essential, especially if he is insufficiently buoyant or if you are in a strong current, high waves or surf.

In changing position, ensure you have an adequate grip before releasing the other hand. You can grip the victim's tank, valve, straps, backpack or buoyancy compensator (being careful not to choke him), but such hand holds are not always available. The tank may have been ditched. If the BC is inflated, it will be more difficult to grip. Thus, you should be accustomed to towing the fellow diver by his limbs, head, and trunk as well as by his gear.

Reassurance for the victim is also important especially if he is verging on panic. Reassure him by talking as well as with eye contact. Consider giving him commands. Get him to help you. Let him know by your voice and your actions that you are in complete control and that he is safe if he does as you say.

Towing efficiency

To avoid potential exhaustion, tow the victim efficiently by increasing propulsion and reducing drag. The greater the rescuer's freedom of movement, the more efficient propulsion will become. Towing a victim while holding him close to your body gives your legs less freedom to kick. However, during any arms-length tow, you may want to periodically draw the victim up next to you to check his face or offer assurance. The arm over arm tow is favored by divers because it allows reasonable freedom of movement for both towing and checking in one continuous operation.

Freedom of movement can be increased by creating a clear area for your fins to kick. If a submersible pressure gauge or octopus regulator tangles your legs, place it over the victim's body or tuck it out of the way.

Most tows leave at least one arm free. With the tired swimmer assist, for example, you can use both of your arms and legs for swimming while the victim holds your shoulders.

Fig. 12-4

Heads out of the water weigh about 8 kg (17 lbs.). In the water, they weigh almost nothing. Keep your ears wet to increase your buoyancy and minimize drag.

If you have not imprisoned his limbs by your towing position, the victim may be able to help propel himself. If you can get helpers, you'll have much greater propulsion.

Reducing drag may be enhanced by weight ditching. This provides more buoyancy, reduces drag by placing the victim in a more horizontal position and reduces the mass you must move through the water.

BCs and inflated suits also increase resistance. Deflate these to the minimum buoyancy you will presumably need. Many BCs increase drag in another way, one that is not generally recognized. While swimming, a large volume of water may collect between the inner bladder and the outer cover. This makes the BC bulkier so that more energy is required to move it through the water.

Fig. 12-5

If you have no landmarks to sight, turn your head and look frequently to be sure you are towing toward safety.

You can also make your tow easier if both you and the victim keep your heads in the water. Not only does this increase your buoyancy and reduce the amount of finning required, but it also places your bodies in a more horizontal position, minimizing drag.

Be sure you are heading towards safety. In some tows, you are facing forward so you can see your objective continuously. In others you are on your back. Unless you are swimming away from landmarks that you can line up to determine your direction, you will have to turn and look occasionally to be sure you are on the right course.

Towing methods

None of the tows described fit every situation. Learn all the methods that seem suited to your diving companions, the gear and the dive sites you normally use. Practice in teams as well as individually, and with victims of different sizes.

Line towing

The quickest way to tow a victim is with a line from a boat or shore. The speed and efficiency of this method are obvious virtues. Moreover, when a line tow with a float is

imminent, there is less need to conserve your strength for the trip back while swimming to the victim.

The first or second rescuer going after the victim should take a line with a float attached. The float, for example; a rescue can or ring buoy, will help support both the victim and rescuer.

Hook one arm through a ring buoy. If necessary, the rescuer can perform artificial respiration. If towed too fast, the rescuer or the victim may become swamped. There is also the danger of pulling the float from the rescuer's grasp or of disrupting the efforts to give air. If a second rescuer controls the victim in the carry and handles the line, these problems are minimized.

Hand signals aid communication between the line handlers and the rescuer. The only standard scuba signals applicable to line towing are "stop" and "slow down."

Any available float-and-line combination can aid a rescue. However, two special buoys and a reel, commonly used by lifeguards, are explicitly made for towing victims through long stretches of rough water.

The rescue tube is made of soft, closed cell foam enclosed in a vinyl skin. The rescue can

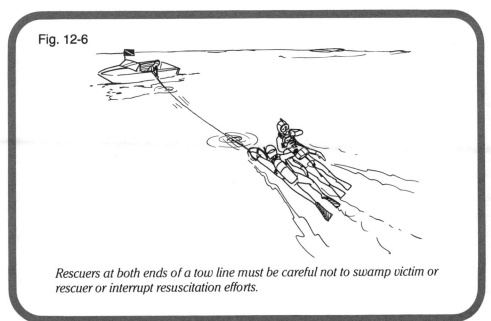

Fig. 12-6

Rescuers at both ends of a tow line must be careful not to swamp victim or rescuer or interrupt resuscitation efforts.

Fig. 12-7

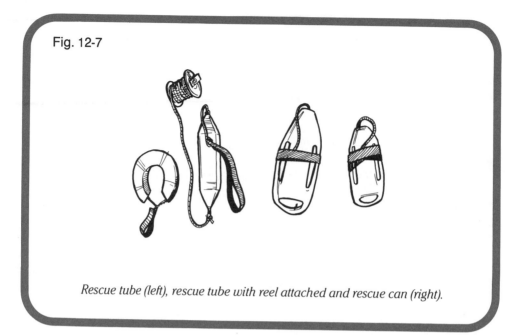

Rescue tube (left), rescue tube with reel attached and rescue can (right).

is a hollow plastic shell with handles. Both these buoyant aids permit attachment of a long line at one end. This line can be tied on before the buoy is launched or carried by a second rescuer. The rescuer places the strap loop over his head and one shoulder allowing both arms to be used for swimming as the victim is towed behind. If a long line is attached to the buoyant aid, the shore or boat rescuers can pull in both victim and rescuer.

If no panic is present, the rescuer may get behind the victim, reach under his arms and grasp the buoy. This way the victim, sandwiched between the rescuer and tube or can,

Fig. 12-8

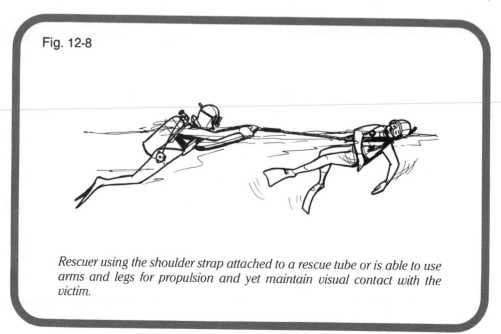

Rescuer using the shoulder strap attached to a rescue tube or is able to use arms and legs for propulsion and yet maintain visual contact with the victim.

Fig. 12-9

Victim can be held between rescuer and tube or can during a long line tow.

will not slip away.

If the victim is passive, a rescue tube can be fastened around him and the long line used to tow both to safety.

Aboard a dive boat, notice the multiplicity of lines you can use for rescue. The best are brightly colored, floatable lines a few hun-

dred meters or yards in length.

There are several ways to make your line ready for instant use. One is to coil it inside a bucket. A small float, fastened to the end of the line, can be placed in the bucket, or the bucket can be placed in an inner tube or ring buoy.

Fig. 12-10

You can fasten a rescue tube around a non-breathing victim and perform rescue breathing, while being towed in on a line.

Fig. 12-11

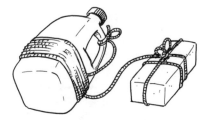

A bucket can be used to store a long line with a buoy attached.

Fig. 12-12

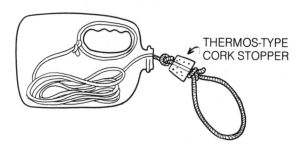

The buoys used as markers for wrecks can be adapted for instant rescue.

Fig. 12-13

THERMOS-TYPE
CORK STOPPER

A plastic bottle rigged this way can be thrown to a victim. The line will pay out as the bottle flies.

The long line with a buoy normally trailed from the stern of a dive boat can be especially useful for divers returning to the boat through a strong current. It can also tow a victim who encounters trouble in its vicinity.

If a victim is close enough and able to grab it firmly, throw him a line—even if no buoy is attached. Stepping on the land end, seize the line and split the coil into two halves, one for each hand. (Lines should be coiled aboard a well-kept boat.) If you throw a half coil, its weight will provide the necessary momentum. Unless tangled, the line will pay off from the other hand. If a buoy is attached, dividing the line is not necessary.

In a wind, aim beyond and to the windward side of the victim.

If you throw wide of the victim, pull the line back quickly, letting the excess drop in a pile along side you. Do not take time to coil it. Retrieve the buoy and throw it again.

A 4 litre or gallon plastic milk bottle makes an excellent buoy for the end of a heaving line. Fill with a small amount of sand or water to give it a little extra weight. Such bottles, already wrapped with a line and a weight attached, are frequently found on dive boats. Both bottle and weight are normally thrown in as marker buoys. For rescue, the weight on the end of the line is secured aboard and the bottle, wrapped with the line, is thrown to the victim.

An alternate way to rig a plastic bottle for rescue is to insert one end of the line, thread it around and through the hollow interior of the handle and secure it with a knot. Next, feed the rest of the line into the bottle, but retain the end and use a bowline knot to make a loop. When a victim in trouble is spotted, the loop is quickly placed over your wrist and the bottle thrown. The interior line gives the bottle sufficient weight and pays out nicely as it sails through the air. The open end is so small that the bottle will not fill with water before the victim can grasp it and be pulled in.

Manufactured "throw bags," used in river rescues, operate on the same principle. A 1 cm or 3/8 in. diameter woven nylon line inside the bag gives weight for throwing and pays out as it flies.

Tired diver assists

The underarm assists are the simplest and

Fig. 12-14

An underarm assist of a calm victim is simple and natural and allows the victim to help you by using his arms and legs for swimming.

most natural way to help a diver who is tired or having difficulty swimming—but first be sure he is unlikely to panic. Place one hand under the tired diver's armpit. Both the victim's arms and legs are free for swimming. The rescuer can swim either face-up or face-down. If you swim face-up, you can better watch and talk to the victim. If you swim face-down, you can better see where you are going.

As a variation, instead of holding the victim at his armpit, grasp his vest or tank strap at the shoulder. Be careful not to choke him.

If available, a second rescuer can assist on the other side of the victim. One rescuer can monitor the victim while the other rescuer steers.

Placing the tired diver's fins against your shoulders and swimming, a rescuer may push the victim. The victim should be face-up whereas the rescuer is face-down. This position is excellent for relieving a cramp in one or both of the victim's legs; the pressure of the rescuer's shoulders against the victim's fins may help to stretch the calf muscles.

In flat calm water, you can use both of your arms for added propulsion. When the water is rough however, both of your hands may be needed to hold the victim's feet against your shoulders. Since the victim's arms are free,

he can use them to swim, maintain balance or remove gear. This position also allows you to watch the victim, talk to him and to see where you are going.

Arm over arm

Used as a tow, the arm over arm is one of the best, especially for an unconscious victim. It offers control and support. You are near the victim's head, which means a good close-up view of his face. You can easily see where you are heading and the tow does not depend on either you or the victim having any equipment.

This method adapts well to two rescuers, one on each side of the victim. If a third is available, he can use the foot push, placing the victim's fins against his shoulders.

Cross chest carry

This tow affords firm support, excellent control and a sense of security for the victim. It is best used when neither you nor the victim is encumbered with gear. The victim's tank will have to be removed. Also, it might be necessary to deflate one or both BCs. You may have to slide your arm under the victim's BC to reach across his chest and grasp his side underneath his far armpit.

Fig. 12-15

A non-panicky victim with cramped calves can be assisted by placing his fins on the rescuer's shoulders.

The arm over arm, one of the best methods, adapts to multiple rescuers.

Tank valve tow

The valve of the victim's tank, or the first stage regulator attached to it, offers an excellent handhold. Accordingly, it is frequently the first thing a rescuer grabs when he starts to tow. (A palm-up grip helps to avoid hand injury if the victim twists.) Some backpacks have a built-in slot near the top which can be used as a handle. A tight grip on the tank straps just above the backpack also provides good control. Your second hand at his armpit will afford added control if needed.

To avoid kicking the victim or his tank, turn sideways, or use a spread-eagle flutter kick with one leg on either side of the victim.

Tank strap tow

A variation of the tank tow—one that offers

Use the two-handed control tow to secure a victim tightly.

Fig. 12-18

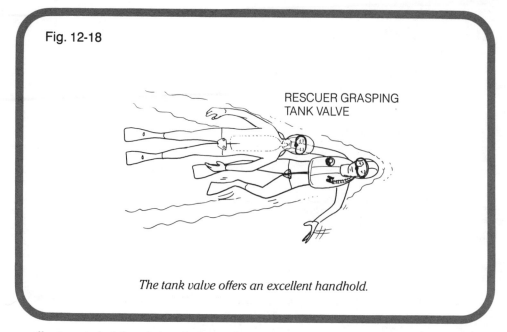

RESCUER GRASPING TANK VALVE

The tank valve offers an excellent handhold.

excellent control of the victim—is the tank-strap tow. Use both hands and grasp the straps on each side of victim's head. His shoulders mark the best points of contact between the straps and your hands.

This tow is especially good for the victim with a suspected neck or back injury, because you can cradle his head between your arms and keep it in line with his body. However, it has the kicking and vision disadvantages of the tank-valve tow, plus an added complication: you cannot turn as far sideways. Naturally, you must use the spread eagle flutter kick, and cannot use your arms for propulsion.

Fig. 12-19

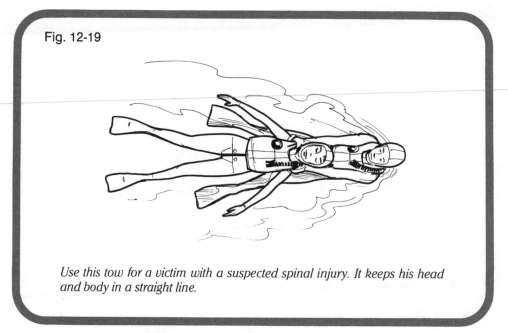

Use this tow for a victim with a suspected spinal injury. It keeps his head and body in a straight line.

Summary

Towing a victim to safety

- Have a firm grasp so you can maintain contact in waves, currents and when there is insufficient buoyancy.
- Reassure the victim.
- Reduce drag and maximize propulsion.
- Obtain assistance from other divers whenever possible.
- Keep checking that the rescuer is on course to safety.
- Rescue cans and tubes, ring buoys and other buoyant aids with attached lines make towing easier for the rescuer.
- There are many towing methods. It is often simplest to grasp the tank valve or backpack handle.
- Where a grasp is made directly with the victim, as opposed to his equipment, the condition of the victim and the environmental hazards will influence the most desirable method of towing.

Rescues using auxiliary equipment

Frequently, some piece of equipment available at the dive site can make a rescue safer, faster and simpler. Examples include extensions, floats, paddleboards, mats and small craft.

Extend your reach

Divers sometimes find themselves in trouble right next to a boat or pier. One excellent way to extend your reach is through the use of lines discussed in Chapter 12. Other extensions include fishing poles, mop handles, boat hooks, spear guns, oars and paddles. Any time such extensions are used, the rescuer should keep his centre of gravity low and brace himself to avoid being pulled into the water.

Floats

Every boat should have floats. The law requires all vessels to carry one approved personal flotation device (PFD) or life jacket per person. These should be kept readily available. Inflatable vests or BCs are not acceptable substitutes.

One or more PFDs can be thrown to a diver in trouble. He will not be able to fit one over his air tank, but he can put it under his arms where it will support him like a pair of water wings.

Many other floatable objects will be aboard your dive boat or at your dive site; these include ring buoys, inner tubes, plastic bottles, insulated coolers, empty gasoline cans or even a wet suit stuffed into a goodie bag. A spare BC can quickly be inflated and thrown to a victim. The strap may be long enough to allow you to pull him in. You can attach any of these items to a line and throw or swim them to a victim for a swift, easy tow back.

Rescue tubes

Frequently carried on small vessels, rescue tubes can be thrown or taken to a victim. The tube can be formed into a ring and used as a towing aid or can be left in its tube shape and used as pictured in Chapter 12.

Inner tube

The inner tubes frequently towed by divers for surface floats can be used for rescue. They offer enough flotation to support two or three fully equipped divers.

An inner tube can furnish plenty of buoyancy for rescue breathing. It is more efficient when the rescuer puts his head and arms through the tube, thus positioning himself above the victim. You can secure the victim's arm by hooking it over the tube. Now apply the arm over arm carry. Different tubes demand different rescue techniques. Practice with the tubes—and the gear—you and your buddies normally use on dives.

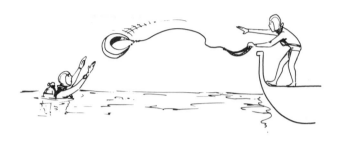

With a line attached, the rescue tube, an inner tube, PFD, BC, etc., can be thrown like a ring buoy.

Paddleboards and surf mats

One of the fastest ways to get to a victim is on a rescue board, paddleboard, surfboard, or surf mat. Many divers use them to reach their dive sites easily. These are available in various sizes. Some have the advantage of being soft and flexible.

A rescuer on a board or mat can skim swiftly over the surface using his arms as paddles. This is probably the easiest way to travel over a kelp bed. By kneeling, the diver can spot a victim above waves and swells and still paddle with his hands.

A regular surfboard is made to hold only one person, and it is much shorter and a little narrower than a rescue board or paddleboard. Accordingly, it has less flotation. It will support either the rescuer or the victim—but not both (unless they are small).

The rescue boards or paddleboards easily support two people, allowing a rescuer to transport a victim quickly by skimming over the surface. However, two fully equipped divers may not be able to mount the board without pushing it at least partially underwater.

Your primary concerns with a motionless victim are to get his face out of the water quickly and to determine if he is breathing. One answer is to position yourself across the board and grasp the victim by reaching over his upper arm and grasping behind his back. You can extend his head with your other hand and clear his airway while you check for breathing. Start rescue breathing if necessary.

Motor boats

You are a safety diver left alone on board a small dive boat while four friends explore the depths. You noticed a diver on the surface three hundred feet down current beyond your trailing drift line. He is trying to reach the buoy at the end of the line, but he obviously can't make it! What will you do?

Boats should have spare lines. Use them to lengthen your drift line, your anchor scope or both. It may not be enough. If you start the motor, you could injure your fellow divers with the propeller. Even if they are too deep to hurt, you do not want them to surface later and find no boat.

Fig. 13-2

An inner tube grabbed suddenly will flip upright unless counterbalanced.

Keep your eye on the victim. Attach a buoy to the anchor line or use a few PFDs. Attach the trailing drift line to the anchor line and let the boat drift clear of the diving area. While drifting, make ready to move by hauling up the ladder or exit platform. Once clear, start the motor and head for the victim. The other divers, when they surface, can hang on to the PFDs, the drift line or the buoy until you return. If you have discussed this contingency with them, they are prepared.

As you approach the drifting victim, shut off the motor and let the boat drift to him. If another diver is aboard, he can keep track of the victim while you maneuver the boat. When close enough, the spotter can throw a PFD or boat cushion, preferably with a line attached. He should also be equipped with diving gear in case the victim sinks. If the victim is rational, ask where his buddy is.

He should also be equipped with diving gear

Fig. 13-3

Get an unconscious victim's face out of the water fast, check for breathing, and commence rescue breathing if required.

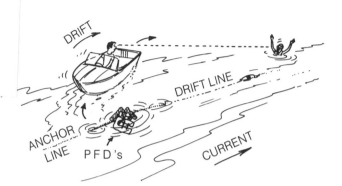

Tie a float to the anchor line and to the drift line so the divers will have something to rest on while waiting for your return.

in case the victim sinks. If the victim is rational, ask where his buddy is.

You should be able to maneuver your boat within reach of an unconscious surface victim. To keep the boat from drifting out of reach, a lone rescuer should not enter the water without connecting himself to the boat with a line.

If the victim is not breathing, commence rescue breathing. Between breaths, shorten the distance between you and the boat by hauling on the line. At the boat, continue rescue breathing holding on to whatever is available—the entry platform, the gunwale, the transom, a line.

On returning to the anchor buoy, stop short of the diving area and wait for an okay signal from the other divers. After all have surfaced,

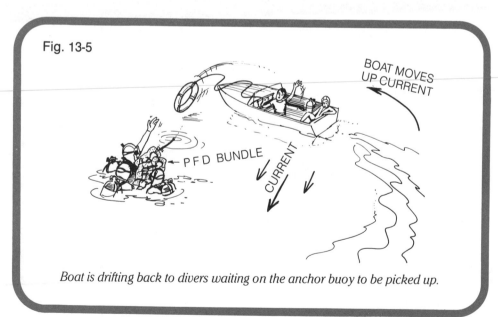

Fig. 13-5

Boat is drifting back to divers waiting on the anchor buoy to be picked up.

Fig. 13-6

In an inflatable boat, you approach a victim directly with minimal danger of injury—assuming ignition is cut.

proceed up-current, cut the motor, and let the boat drift back to the anchor buoy. Throw a line, if necessary, to make contact with the waiting divers. Then, secure the boat to the anchor line as the divers climb aboard.

Inflatable boats

The major advantages of inflatables for rescue are their stability and low freeboard. The soft sides make injury to the victim unlikely. Accordingly, a victim may be approached directly. To avoid a propeller wound, cut the ignition before getting too close. Rescue techniques are similar to those described for motor boats.

Other small craft

Any small craft can aid in a scuba rescue; rowboats, sailboats, canoes, paddle boats, swan boats, kayaks, houseboats, cabin cruisers, pontoon boats, and jet skis require techniques similar to those described for more conventional craft. Specific adaptations can be learned through practice.

If you are going to operate any such unit in a scuba diving area, be prepared to rescue a diver. To determine how well it will work, stage a simulated accident.

Summary

Know how to use auxiliary equipment in order to make a faster and safer rescue

Floats, rescue tubes and cans, inner tubes, paddleboards, rescue boards and surfboards make the rescue simpler for both rescuer and victim. Any small craft can be useful in an emergency if it is properly equipped and if the operator can safely maneuvre the craft.

Removing a victim from the water

General principles

Hauling a limp, heavy, unconscious victim onto a boat, through heavy surf, waves, or onto a jagged, rocky shore, all the while breathing for him, is close to impossible for a lone rescuer. Much of this information assumes that help is available—something you should have considered *before entering* the water.

In an emergency, enlist anyone who is near the dive site, not just the members of your party. Too often potential helpers stand around watching a rescuer struggle because they do not know what they can do. Tell them. Assistants in the water can bring floats and lines, remove gear, or spell you on rescue breathing. Call for help early and often.

Even non-swimmers can throw floats and lines, pull you in, and aid in the lifting operation. After removing a victim's heavy gear, two on-shore helpers, each grasping an arm, can remove a victim with less effort since each will be pulling only half of the victim's weight. They may also rig a line or net for easier lifting onto a high deck.

Fig. 14-1

Multiple rescuers make lifting easier by dividing a victim's weight between them.

Fig. 14-2

As soon as you can do so with assurance, check carotid pulse.

Remember to check airway, breathing, and circulation; check the carotid pulse of a breathing victim the second you reach shallow water or the side of the boat. You will not be able to feel a pulse through wet suit material; unzip the victim's jacket and fold back the hood. Since you may be exhausted from towing, numb from cold, and have hands encumbered by gloves, have someone else check the pulse if possible.

If he has no pulse, get him out of the water and onto a hard, flat surface so you can give CPR.

Rescue the rescuer. After a long, arduous tow, he is going to be tired and vulnerable. Do not forget to account for the buddies of both victim and rescuer.

Fig. 14-3

As you remove the victim from the water, position him to allow fluids to drain. If victim is not breathing, take only a few seconds.

Perhaps the victim should not be taken out of the water immediately. Unless his heart has stopped, getting him out of the water quickly is not nearly as important as keeping him breathing and getting him out carefully without causing further injury.

If you are faced with towing a victim through heavy surf, it may be best to wait beyond the surf line for a rescue boat.

Injuries add special complications to the removal operation. However, the surrounding water reduces a victim's weight and supports his body; it acts as a kind of splint. Fractures and dislocations are aggravated out of the water as gravity pulls on them. Thus, splint all broken or dislocated limbs prior to removal. If compound fractures are not immobilized before the victim is exposed to normal gravity, the jagged bone edges are liable to cause a more extensive injury. If you suspect a spinal injury, secure the victim on a spine board.

Remove heavy gear before trying to get a victim out of the water. The victim's tank and weight belt should be taken off if this was not done en route. Whenever attempting to lift anyone, use your leg muscles to avoid injuring the less powerful back muscles.

As the victim is lifted from the water, if his mouth can be positioned lower than his chest, water will tend to drain out of his airway.

When the victim is lowered, take advantage of any inclines—a sloping beach or boat deck—and position his head lower than his body. This helps drain fluids and tends to concentrate blood in the upper body. If the victim is unconscious but breathing, use the coma position, with the legs elevated slightly higher than the head, left side down.

Small Boats

You are holding on to the transom of a boat, administering rescue breathing. Between breaths, you have checked and removed your own and the victim's gear.

Fig. 14-4

Hook the victim's arms over the transom and hold them as you climb aboard.

Now how do you get him aboard? Hook his arms over the transom, crossed, so you can hold them with one hand as you climb in. Your fins will help to give you the momentum you need to get over the transom. Keep holding his arms as you climb into the boat.

Use a straight arm lift. Grasp the victim's arms. Brace yourself. Dunk the victim momentarily, if necessary, in order to provide upward momentum, then lift straight up until his waist bends over the top of the tran-

Fig. 14-5

Grasp the victim's arms, lift straight up until his waist bends over the transom.

Fig. 14-6

Shift your hands to the victim's waist and pull his hips over the transom.

and ventilate immediately. If he is breathing, place him in the coma position. If the victim is not breathing and you were unable to check his pulse previously, do so now. If you detect no pulse, start CPR immediately.

To assist a victim who is only slightly incapacitated, hang on to the gunwale or transom and duck underwater, extending your arms. He can use your shoulders as an underwater step.

A line strung over the side from bow to stern will serve as a foot step. If you failed to do this before leaving the boat, try rigging the anchor line. Another method is to provide a stirrup by hanging a secured bowline loop over the side.

som. Now shift your hands to his waist, or grasp his BC waist strap, being careful that his head does not strike the deck or seat. Carefully lift and pull his hips over the transom.

Finally, if the victim is still not breathing, turn him face up at the bottom of the boat

Fig. 14-8

A line from bow to stern will serve as a foot step.

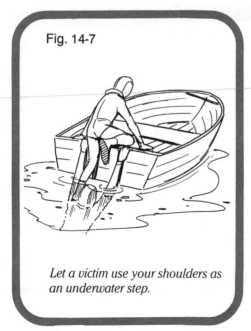

Fig. 14-7

Let a victim use your shoulders as an underwater step.

The cavitation plate above the propeller of an outboard motor looks like a handy place to step. Do not be tempted: you could be badly cut if your foot slipped off the plate and you fell into the sharp propeller.

To aid reentry, many dive boats have a wide, water-level platform at the stern. In calm water, assuming you have no help, you can swim a victim up to the platform, cross his arms on it and hold him with one hand as you climb on. A straight arm lift can then be used to get the victim onto the platform.

Fig. 14-9

Use a bowline loop as a "stirrup" to climb aboard.

If the water is rough, approach the rocking platform cautiously. Call for help from those on board. Keep the victim between you and the platform, mooring yourself with a stern line if available. Now, study the oscillations. Push the victim onto the platform as it drops underwater and hold him there securely so he is not swept off as the surge reverses. On the next surge you can wash yourself aboard and hold fast.

Fig. 14-10

Cross victim's arms on the platform and hold them as you climb on.

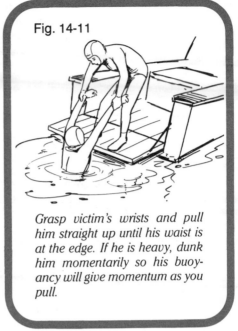

Fig. 14-11

Grasp victim's wrists and pull him straight up until his waist is at the edge. If he is heavy, dunk him momentarily so his buoyancy will give momentum as you pull.

Fig. 14-12

Protecting his head, bend his torso forward and hold him as you release his wrists and pull his legs onto the platform.

Net roll-up

With large boats and an unconscious, injured or exhausted victim, the rescuer needs a technique that will reduce the force required to raise the victim over the side.

If a two hundred pound victim is placed in a looped net and two people roll him up, the one hundred pound pull will be divided between them. Each will be lifting only about fifty pounds.

An ideal net can be made for your dive boat as diagrammed. The bars make it easy for one person to roll a victim aboard. First, one end of the net is tied to the gunwale. Alternatively, the rescuers can secure the end by standing on it.

The net is placed in the water so that the bars fastened to the net will be on the top (facing away from the side of the boat). The lower bars are of metal so they will sink the net, allowing the victim to be positioned, lying face up on the bars, by a rescuer in the water.

The victim is rolled up by pulling on the ropes, on the bars attached to the ropes, on the pole, and then on the bars attached to the net. The hauler's hand should reach inside for each new grip so that ropes, pole and bars all end up outside of the net instead of tangled inside on top of the victim.

Rope roll-up

Any rope or line aboard can be rigged to obtain the same mechanical advantage. Two persons, using the lines as shown in Figure 14-15, can easily lift a victim from the water.

Secure both ends of each line to something stable inside the boat gunwale. If this is impossible, tie "stop knots" in the lines. The two haulers stand with a foot on each of the four ends, grasping the two lines at their midpoints. The two pairs of loops thus formed drop into the water. The arrangement works best when the lines are of sinkable material. Viewed from the front, they form a pair of W's.

An in-water rescuer positions the loops around the victim. One loop is placed under the victim's upper back, one under his waist, one under the mid thighs and one under the calves. As each loop is placed, it should be tightened so it will not come loose as the others are positioned. The victim's arms should be kept inside the loops, and care taken that the line under his upper back does not slip toward his neck. To avoid this, the line must drop vertically from the gunwale to the victim's upper back. If it is angled down, it will invariably slip under his neck as he is rolled up. With the lines set correctly, pull carefully on the loops, hand over hand. Watch the victim to synchronize your efforts. Keep him level—or slightly head-down. In seconds he will be atop the gunwale. If you have stepped on the lines, remember not to lift your feet until the victim is safely on board. Obviously the in-water rescuer should stay clear as the victim is rolled up, but be ready to retrieve him if he drops.

Fig. 14-13

If the victim is rolled up by two rescuers, each will be lifting only one-quarter of the victim's weight.

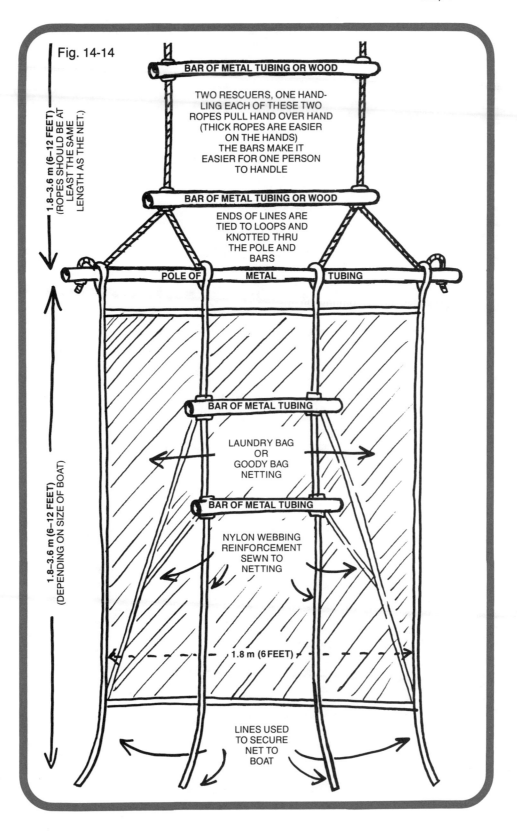

Fig. 14-14

1.8–3.6 m (6–12 FEET) (ROPES SHOULD BE AT LEAST THE SAME LENGTH AS THE NET.)

BAR OF METAL TUBING OR WOOD

TWO RESCUERS, ONE HAND-LING EACH OF THESE TWO ROPES PULL HAND OVER HAND (THICK ROPES ARE EASIER ON THE HANDS) THE BARS MAKE IT EASIER FOR ONE PERSON TO HANDLE

BAR OF METAL TUBING OR WOOD

ENDS OF LINES ARE TIED TO LOOPS AND KNOTTED THRU THE POLE AND BARS

POLE OF METAL TUBING

1.8–3.6 m (6–12 FEET) (DEPENDING ON SIZE OF BOAT)

BAR OF METAL TUBING

LAUNDRY BAG OR GOODY BAG NETTING

BAR OF METAL TUBING

NYLON WEBBING REINFORCEMENT SEWN TO NETTING

1.8 m (6 FEET)

LINES USED TO SECURE NET TO BOAT

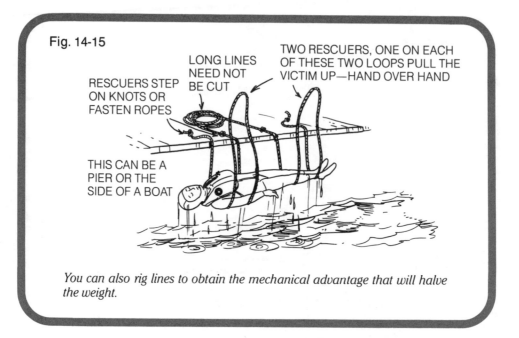

Fig. 14-15

RESCUERS STEP ON KNOTS OR FASTEN ROPES

LONG LINES NEED NOT BE CUT

TWO RESCUERS, ONE ON EACH OF THESE TWO LOOPS PULL THE VICTIM UP—HAND OVER HAND

THIS CAN BE A PIER OR THE SIDE OF A BOAT

You can also rig lines to obtain the mechanical advantage that will halve the weight.

If there is only one rescuer on board, and the lines are secured to the gunwale, he can easily control the victim by keeping the lines or net snug while the in-water rescuer climbs out to help pull.

If the victim is conscious and able to follow your instructions by placing the loops under himself, you will be able to roll him up unassisted. Secure the lines so they will not slip from under your feet. Use two loops, one in the middle of the victim's back and one under the middle of his thighs. He must remain stiff as you roll him up.

This obviously will not work for a limp, unconscious victim. A one-person roll-up works better with a net, since body stiffening is not required and a conscious victim can more easily position himself. But a rescuer will be needed in the water if the victim is unconscious.

Bowline lifts

Some boats have a block-and-tackle or winch that makes hauling a heavy victim aboard easy. If the winch is used, coordinate everyone's actions and communicate with the winch operator, who probably cannot see the victim. To use a winch, you must secure the

victim in such a way that he will not be squeezed to death by the line (as could happen with a slip knot, for instance) or fall out if the knot loosens. The bowline is the knot of choice.

Fig. 14-16

A conscious victim who can keep his body stiff can be lifted this way by one person.

Fig. 14-17

THE BOWLINE.

Fig. 14-18

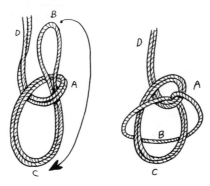

THE BOWLINE ON A BIGHT.

Fig. 14-19

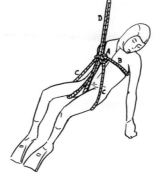

LIFTING AN UNCONSCIOUS VICTIM WITH A BOWLINE ON A BIGHT.

Fig. 14-20

When taking an unconscious victim up a ladder, you must keep your knee higher than your groin so the victim will not slide off your thigh.

Ladder carries

If a victim is lighter than the rescuer, the rescuer may be able to carry the unconscious victim up a ladder. The ladder must be strong, stiff, and it must extend into the water far enough to get a foot on the bottom rung with the victim supported by the rescuer.

Remove all encumbering gear from the victim and yourself including fins. Put the victim's head on your shoulder facing you. Put your arms under his arms and grasp the sides of the ladder.

Place one of your legs between the victim's legs and your foot high on a rung so the victim ends up sitting on your thigh. Keep your knee higher than your groin with your thigh angled up so that if the victim slides, he will come toward you and snug against your body.

Climb the ladder by bringing your other foot up to the same rung as your first foot, which can then be moved up one rung. Repeat this procedure, always keeping the leg on which the victim is resting high. Keep grasping the ladder with both hands, slide your hands up the sides.

If you can insert your arms with the victim's through the armholes of a wrap-around BC, you can use it as a backpack to carry the victim, hands free.

Fig. 14-21

If you can insert your arms through the armholes of a wrap-around BC, you can use it as a backpack to carry the victim, hands free.

Jettison his weight system and tank. This should have been done already. But if not, do not neglect to disconnect his low pressure inflator hose first. Make sure his waist strap buckle is secure. Deflate his BC so you will have room for both your arms and his, then insert your arms as if you were donning a coat. Lean forward so the victim's weight is primarily on your back and climb the ladder. Remember, once you start up, do not let go of the ladder.

Surf

Breaking waves create surf, a water environment that is unlike any other. Depending on the time, the place and especially the wind, surf can be gentle or highly dangerous.

General considerations

As high waves break, tons of water can slam you against the bottom, which may contain hard sand, broken shells, barnacle-covered rocks, jagged coral formations, spiny sea urchins or man-made structures. The wise diver steers clear of such obstructions, waits out the high waves and gets through the surf zone as quickly as possible especially when handling a victim.

A wave breaks when a shallow bottom interferes with its motion, so that the top of the wave pitches forward. Waves breaking off shore indicate a reef, sand bar or other obstruction.

Conversely, a persistent gap in a line of breakers could mean deeper water through which a rip current is pouring seaward. You might use a rip current for a quick ride out to rescue someone beyond the surf line, but you do not want to swim through one when you are heading for shore. Swim to the side out of the current.

Become experienced in surf conditions, first as a swimmer, then as a snorkeler, before entering it wearing scuba gear. Become accustomed to gentle surf first.

Waves come in all sizes but they usually follow a pattern. After a "set" of big ones hits, there is frequently a hiatus consisting of much smaller waves. Then a big set returns. The experienced diver times these cycles and enters the surf just as a big set is waning.

Saving a life when either you or the victim is wearing full gear poses many problems in calm water. In even moderate surf, these problems are enormously multiplied; so before bringing a victim to shore through the surf line, jettison all unnecessary gear.

Think about your buoyancy. The large cross section of a fully inflated BC may cause you to be buffeted by the waves. Or its buoyancy may float you so high you go "over the falls" and are dashed against the bottom. Maybe you should let out some air.

Control the victim by holding him tightly. The arm over arm tow allows you to watch the oncoming waves and turn the victim so they do not slam him in the face. If he is unconscious, you can cover his mouth and nose so he does not inhale water.

Fig. 14-22

Use a rip current for a quick ride out to rescue a victim, but don't try to swim back in that way.

If help is on the way, your best option might be to wait outside the surf line with the victim. Or, if you found him in the surf, consider taking him seaward until your help arrives. It may be in the form of a boat which could minimize your problems. If swimmers come to your aid, they can help you tow.

Do not try to give a victim air while taking him through heavy surf. If possible, while still outside the surf line, ventilate him thoroughly with a few quick, full breaths. Then, following a receding set of large waves, cradle his head, cover his mouth and nose with your hand and drive through the surf zone as quickly as possible. When you reach calmer shallows, give the victim another series of quick, full breaths. After you have brought the victim up a beach far enough that you will not be disturbed by waves, check his carotid pulse. If his heart has stopped, immediately get him to a hard, flat surface and give CPR.

Surf beach rescue

You are relaxing on the beach when you notice a diver coming in through the surf. He manages to stand up in the shallows just as a big breaker crashes into his back and knocks him down. As he struggles to his feet, another wave smacks him down and he all but disappears in the foam. Tired, out of air, numb with cold, burdened with gear, the diver cannot effectively deal with tons of water crashing against him every few seconds.

What should you do from the beach? Two or three rescuers can handle such a victim more easily than one. Call for help, but you need not wait until help arrives. Even without any gear, you can attempt to rescue the victim.

Watch him so you do not lose him; watch the waves so you do not get dumped. During a lull, drop his weight belt, grab his tank valve

and help him to his *knees* (not to his feet!). Then, still holding the valve, steady him while telling him to crawl up out of the surf. You can help him by pulling forward on the tank, but do not lift it so he loses traction for crawling.

Any available assistants can help by removing victim's gear. Use the wave movement to float the victim quickly up the beach. If all else fails, he may be rolled up the slope.

An inexperienced diver entering the water through *heavy* surf is asking for trouble. Warning signs of a potential victim include:

— Entering with a fully inflated BC. He will not be able to dive under the waves.
— Starting into breakers before fully donning mask. A wave may tear the mask away.
— Carrying flippers instead of wearing them. He may lose them, or be unable to don them to swim out of the surf zone quickly.
— Stopping in the surf zone to adjust gear and, therefore, not watching the waves.
— Walking forward with fins on.
— Allowing waves to hit him broadside.
— Falling, tumbling and losing gear.

Any of these behaviors should make you anticipate a rescue. You may be able to bring him in as you would an exiting diver.

There is an important difference between a floundering diver entering the water and a floundering diver leaving the water. If the relatively untired diver fumbles while entering the water, but finally gets his act together, he will probably disappear completely and use his regulator to swim out under the waves. By contrast, if a floundering diver disappears trying to *leave* the water, he is probably in trouble and needs to be rescued.

Rescuing any diver incapacitated on the bottom in the surf zone is difficult. The situation calls for a quick assessment including the equipment you should or should not be wearing.

For shallow bottom searches, some surf lifeguards take not only a mask, snorkel, and fins, but also a small bottle of compressed air. This allows them to cover a much larger area than they could without any air, but unencumbered by a full size tank. Thus, a pony bottle that is easily removed from your rig can be a useful piece of rescue equipment on a beach dive.

Another item useful for surf emergencies is the rescue tube, especially, if a line connects it to a reel on shore.

Rocky shore

Landing a victim in an area with large rocks is difficult but not necessarily as dangerous as one might think. If the waves are not crashing *over* the rocks, the water as it rebounds will tend to keep you from being dashed hard against them.

As you tow the victim close, watch the waves and try to ride a swell up onto a rock ledge. Hold the victim sideways and push him onto it in front of you. As the wave recedes from the ledge, brace yourself and hold on to avoid both being swept away. During the lull, crawl upward with the victim, then brace yourself again. If the next swell floats you higher, brace and hold as before, then resume the climb. If you called for help while on your way to the victim, others may be there to assist you in getting him off the rocks.

Otherwise, after removing your fins and any other encumbering gear, proceed up cau-

tiously, watching for slippery algae, sharp surfaces, holes, and surprise waves. One of the simplest and safest methods of getting the victim onto high ground if the shore is smooth enough is to slide your arms under the victim's and clasp your hands around the victim's chest, then drag him. If you are not strong enough to drag the victim and the shoreline is smooth, you may progress by alternately standing and falling backwards with him.

Shallow water

If you are not in heavy waves, removing a victim from shallow water is relatively easy. But you must still contend with the victim's enormously greater weight out of the water. An underarm drag is normally the simplest initial solution because part of the victim's weight stays in the water. You can walk backwards with your fins on.

If he is waist deep, the victim can easily be lifted from the underarm drag into a saddleback carry because most of his weight will remain underwater. Also, your low center of gravity gives you more stability. If you walk backwards, you can leave your fins on until you are ready to lay the victim down.

Another way of carrying a victim is the backpack carry—on your back with his arms over

Fig. 14-23

The saddleback carry gives you a low centre of gravity with most of the victim's weight supported by the water.

Fig. 14-24

After your fins are removed, you can transport the victim using the backpack carry.

your shoulders. This is best accomplished after your fins have been removed. Is a second rescuer available? Before either of you stand up, he can remove your fins and his own, then lift the victim's legs, thus, reducing the weight you are carrying.

If you are administering mouth-to-snorkel breathing, switch to mouth-to-mouth as soon as you reach calm, shallow water. You should be able to stand on the bottom and give air easily without getting water in the victim's mouth. Grasp the victim under his near arm and support his back with your thigh. Check the victim's carotid pulse, as soon as possible, and get him to a hard, flat surface immediately if CPR is required.

Summary

Assistance is usually essential in order to remove a victim from the water

- Enlist the aid of potential helpers.
- Remove gear in order to make the victim lighter and easier to handle.
- Continue to monitor the victim's condition during removal.
- It may be necessary to wait until appropriate equipment and/or assistants are available in order to complete a safe removal.

Techniques for getting a victim into a boat or onto a pier are:

- Lifting a victim into a small boat.
- Rolling a victim up to the level of a gunwale by means of a net or ropes
- Bowline lifts
- Ladder carries

WHEN DEPARTING FROM SURF, time your exit to avoid being driven into the bottom or onto rocks.

IN SHALLOW CALM WATER, grasping under the victim's arms and dragging him while walking backwards is a popular technique. The saddleback and backpack carries are also useful under acceptable conditions.

Emergency care on deck or shore

15

This chapter summarizes the priorities in emergency care related to diving. Divers are referred to any of the excellent first aid texts currently available for details of general first aid.

Assessment

Determine the extent of the problem. Use all your senses—LOOK, LISTEN and FEEL. The examination of the victim should follow the format of first and second priority for all acutely ill victims.

First priority

A rapid assessment to detect life-threatening disorders of:

A–Airway   Is there evidence of any obstruction?

B–Breathing   Despite an open airway, is the victim in respiratory distress, ie. labored breathing, venting rapidly, demonstrating air hunger, etc.?
Look, listen and feel for injuries to the chest.

C–Circulation   Is there a carotid pulse? Fast or slow? Weak or strong?
Are the arms and legs well perfused with blood, or cool and pale?
Any bleeding sites?

D–Disability of nervous system   Assess the pupils (size, reaction to light) and mental status. Is the victim alert? Does he respond to questions? Is he unconscious?

Second priority

A look, listen and feel assessment of the entire body from head to toe:

    Head and face
    Neck and spine
    Chest
    Abdomen
    Hips, arms and legs
    Neurological examination (see method in this Chapter)

This determination should be a standard examination which is not easily forgotten in a stressful situation. Others involved in the accident may be able to supply information concerning the accident.

Call or send for help

Call or radio a rescue agency and inform them of the accident. An inexpensive CB radio is valuable for this purpose. Give your exact location and any identifying features of your dive boat or dive site. Request hyperbaric chamber personnel or a medical facility to expect you.

Get bystanders to help manage the victim. They can control bleeding, clear vomit, remove false teeth, fashion and apply splints, remove gear, loosen clothing, dry and cover the victim, and make him comfortable. If qualified, they can assist with CPR.

To be certain that someone gets help, make eye contact with a specific individual and tell him exactly what to do. "Bill, call the Coast Guard!" Or "Ann, get an ambulance!"

Do no further harm

You have determined the extent of the problem and sent for the appropriate help. The victim should now be protected in order that his condition will not become worse.

First aid measures should be commenced based upon the injury and the rescuer's capabilities to deal with the injury.

Remove the victim from potential risks; water, sun, wind, cold, heat, fire, gas, blowing sand, exhaust fumes, sharp or jagged surfaces, etc.

Remove potential harm from the victim—airway obstructions (water, vomit, mud, sand, chewing gum, false teeth, regulator or snorkel mouthpiece nibs), obstructions to chest expansion (tight clothing, buoyancy compensator, wet suit, weight belt or tank straps), obstructions to circulation (instrument straps, rubber bands, tight wet suit or clothing), toxic material (venomous tentacles, poisonous spines, corrosive liquids).

Be gentle, calm and reasoning.

Never attempt to recompress a victim by submerging.

Treat for shock

A victim of any accident is likely to develop shock. This term refers to an inadequate blood perfusion of all organs and tissues resulting in the simultaneous depression of many key body functions. Shock can threaten life even when the injury is not in itself lethal. Early signs of shock are weakness, pale or bluish skin (often cold and clammy), a weak but rapid pulse, severe thirst, restlessness, and nausea with vomiting.

Anticipate shock following any accident. Prevent it by treating for it before any symptoms appear. Eliminate the cause of the injury if possible. Then aim toward improving circulation, supplying adequate oxygen and maintaining body temperature.

Keep the victim lying down, dry, with legs elevated, and body covered to prevent loss of body heat.

Use common sense to determine the amount of insulation for a diver in shock. On a cool day the wet suit is best left on, but unzipped (openings covered) with straps loosened to allow easy breathing. If it is very cold, the victim will need additional cover, underneath as well as on top. Extra wet suits (preferably dry) can be used if blankets are not available.

If the day is uncomfortably hot, a wet suit jacket may be gently removed. Cut the jacket off if necessary, using your sharp diving knife cautiously. Lubricate rubber with water to make cutting easier. The wet suit pants are better left on to restrict blood flow to this region and thereby increase the amount available for the brain. Pull "Farmer John" type high-waisted pants down below the rib cage to allow easy breathing.

 **A victim of near-drowning revives quickly, gets up, thanks you for saving his life and leaves hurriedly. He is feeling so embarrassed by his failure to cope that he wants to put it all behind him.**

Do not let him get up, much less walk away. He is probably suffering from shock and should be treated accordingly. Also, anyone who has been unconscious in the water may have inhaled water and could suffer delayed effects. The victim must be taken to a medical facility where he can be placed under constant observation and receive appropriate treatment.

Problems specific to diving (Bubble trouble)

This diver surfaced alongside the boat and climbed aboard with help. He staggered a bit while removing heavy gear. (We all do on a rocking boat.) He panted (apparently from the exertion) and coughed a lot. He fumbled trying to remove the regulator from his tank and didn't respond when asked if he needed help. Finally he gave up, rubbed his eyes, mumbled something about a headache and being tired, and collapsed on the deck.

A strenuous dive often makes a person cold, numb and weak. But this diver has exhibited many signs of either air embolism or decompression sickness—coughing, shortness of breath, poor balance, headache, fatigue, blurred vision, impaired hearing, speech difficulties, and possible loss of consciousness. (The trouble signs are diverse because bubbles—whether caused initially by lung rupture or by inadequate decompression—can lodge almost anywhere in the body.) Cessation of breathing and cardiac arrest could follow.

Air embolism

The bubbles of air embolism are more dangerous than those of decompression sickness because they commonly block blood supplying the heart and brain. If a bubble lodges in the artery feeding the heart, the effect is similar to a heart attack. If it stops in a vessel serving the brain, it will trigger symptoms of a stroke. The deprived portion of the brain and what it controls will be seriously impaired or cease to function.

Usually more than one bubble is involved. Sometimes the bubbles are so numerous that the autopsied brain resembles a swiss cheese.

When the bubbles lodge in only one hemisphere of the brain, only one side of the body is affected. Compare the functions on the left side of the body with those on the right. Brain dysfunction may also cause a behavioral or personality change. Make a complete neurological evaluation described at the end of this section.

The onset of air embolism is usually sudden and dramatic. It often occurs within seconds after surfacing. The questions raised by minor symptoms are frequently resolved by the swift appearance of severe dysfunctions: blindness, unequal pupils, loss of hearing or speech, chest pains, paralysis, convulsions, or unconsciousness with respiratory or cardiac arrest. Any signs appearing more than a quarter-hour after the victim surfaces are more likely the bends, and not air embolism.

If your "sleeping" diver is actually unconscious (you cannot wake him), assume air embolism. If he awakens, keep him lying down. Ask what happened. Remember, if he breathed air from any source underwater at a depth beyond 1.2 m (4 ft.), he may have a ruptured lung.

If air embolism is even suspected, place the victim in the coma position with legs elevated, give oxygen if available and make arrangements to transport to a hyperbaric chamber, NO MATTER HOW FAR AWAY. Monitor his vital signs en route.

Pneumothorax

If the air escaping from ruptured lung lodges between the lungs and the chest wall, pneumothorax results. As this air expands, the lung on that side gets smaller and may collapse. This condition may even displace the heart and its connecting vessels reducing blood circulation.

The victim's skin, lips and fingernail beds may become cyanotic. He will breathe more rapidly to compensate. But in this condition deep breaths hurt, so he will breathe shallowly and may bend toward the side involved to ease the pain. His chest will expand unevenly.

If you suspect pneumothorax, loosen anything that restricts breathing, have the victim lie quietly with the affected side down, administer oxygen if available, and elevate the legs (unless this causes breathing difficulty). A mild case may quickly become life-threatening. If he stops breathing, start rescue breathing, but gently to avoid increasing the volume of trapped air. Obtain medical assistance without delay.

Pneumothorax, especially one which progressively enlarges, is a life-threatening emergency and must be treated as soon as possible at the nearest hospital. Because of the association in diving injuries of pneumothorax with air embolism, consideration should also be given to the possibility of both injuries occurring concurrently and the urgent need for therapy at a hyperbaric chamber.

A neurological examination may detect subtle signs of neurological damage from air embolism and the resulting need for hyperbaric chamber treatment. However, the treatment of respiratory distress from pneumothorax takes precedence over all other injuries and longer transport times to a hyperbaric chamber should not be undertaken until the respiratory distress has been stabilized.

Mediastinal emphysema

Air in the midline of the chest, mediastinal emphysema, is another lung overpressure possibility. The misplaced air may produce pain under the breastbone (which may radiate to the neck or shoulder), faintness, shortness of breath and cyanosis.

Give the victim oxygen, if available, and place him in a recovery or coma position with legs elevated slightly unless this causes breathing difficulties.

Although mediastinal emphysema is not usually life-threatening, watch the victim for more serious problems. Conduct a neurological evaluation. Immediately obtain medical assistance, preferably a physician trained in diving accidents, since air embolism or pneumothorax may also be present. A medical facility where the victim's condition can be monitored continuously and where he can be recompressed, if necessary, would be ideal.

Subcutaneous emphysema

Air trapped under the skin, subcutaneous emphysema, usually in the vicinity of the neck or collarbone, is easily confirmed. The neck will be swollen, possibly causing a squeaky voice and difficulty in breathing or swallowing. More importantly a crackling will be heard and felt when the skin is moved. This crackling is such a clear sign of lung overpressure that you should immediately feel the neck area of anyone who experiences distress right after a dive.

Give oxygen if available, and place the victim in the coma position with legs elevated (unless this increases breathing difficulty). Conduct a neurological evaluation and watch the victim for possible complications of air embolism or pneumothorax. Obtain medical assistance immediately—preferably a physician who knows diving medicine. A medical facility with a hyperbaric chamber is the best destination for this victim.

Decompression sickness (Bends)

The diver who develops symptoms after climbing aboard is more likely to be suffering from decompression sickness than from air embolism. Because the neurological symptoms may be similar, it is sometimes difficult even for diving physicians to make an accurate diagnosis. When in doubt, assume air embolism.

Sometimes a diver, after surfacing with a sore

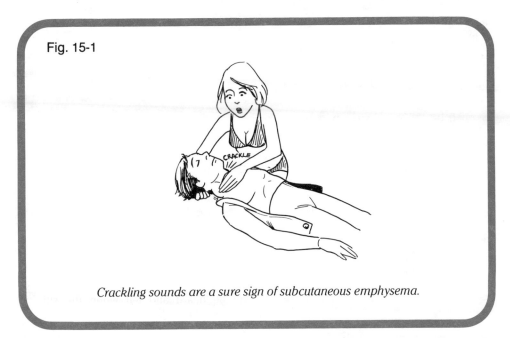

Crackling sounds are a sure sign of subcutaneous emphysema.

spot, will be unsure if it was caused by the bends or by a mechanical injury. Squeezing the area may give a hint. The pain of bends will not intensify with pressure.

Although the onset of bends symptoms occurs within 30 minutes in 50% of cases and within 3 hours for 95% of cases, some victims first experience problems as long as 24 hours after diving.

Decompression sickness appears in two forms, Type I and Type II. A victim suffering from pain, itching, skin rash, or excessive fatigue is classified as a Type I case even though the pain in his bone muscles or joints may be intense and deep. Type II symptoms include neurological dysfunction, paralysis (or other indications of spinal cord damage), dizziness (also known as "the staggers"), breathlessness (also known as "the chokes"), collapse, and unconsciousness. Make a complete neurological evaluation. There may be *severe* decompression sickness (or air embolism) without *any* pain.

First aid for Type I bends, for Type II bends and for air embolism is similar. Place the victim in the coma position, administer oxygen if available, and transport him to a hyperbaric chamber. Victims with only mild symptoms should be watched for signs of serious bends. The victims of both air embolism and bends should be checked for neurological problems and watched for such complications as vomiting, unconsciousness, breathing difficulties and cardiac arrest. CPR may be necessary.

Two aspirin tablets and *plenty* of water to drink (one litre within an hour) are recommended for any bends victim who can swallow. Fruit juices can be given but no alcoholic or carbonated drinks. The clotting mechanism is triggered by gas bubbles inside the bloodstream, making them larger, sticky and more likely to obstruct small blood vessels. The oral fluids and aspirin help to minimize this.

A victim with only mild bends symptoms, such as skin itch, should be kept cool, lying down, and given oxygen. Exercise, massage or heat should be avoided. Attempt to keep the victim alert.

Even if the symptoms disappear, continue first aid measures all the way to the hyperbaric chamber.

Only the bubble—not the clotted blood around it—can be made smaller by recompression. Therefore a diver with bubble trouble should not only be recompressed but also be given medical treatment designed to eliminate residual problems.

It has been found that divers who approach the no-decompression limits can develop bubbles in their blood even if they exhibit no symptoms of the bends. Although apparently tolerated by the body, such bubbles could have unknown long term effects. If you want to be safe: Dive conservatively so you do not form *any* bubbles. Keep well hydrated and avoid strenuous activity for an hour after surfacing.

Neurological evaluation

Serious damage to the brain or spinal cord can result from either air embolism or decompression sickness. However symptoms of such injury may not be immediately apparent and are often overlooked or ignored. A systematic neurological examination by a trained physician takes about thirty minutes and requires certain diagnostic equipment. However, a preliminary neurological examination requiring no special equipment can be administered by non-medical persons.

During the examination, make a particular note of any deviations from normal and record these facts. If you cannot complete any part of the assessment, go to the next step, but note the reason for the omission. Avoid the temptation to omit certain parts (such as orientation to time, place, and person) because the victim "isn't in that bad shape." You may get a surprise!

Dick Clarke, the Senior Saturation Diving Superintendent for Oceaneering International, designed the following examination with the help of neurologists at the University of Southern California. It takes about four minutes to complete. A sport diver would only do this if the time and personnel were available. Remember, transport to a hyperbaric chamber is the first priority! Complete this examination while waiting or en route.

1. Mental: Test the victim's orientation to time, place, and person by asking him what day it is, what time of day, who he is, and where he is. Note the appropriate responses to all of the questions asked in the evaluations which follow.

2. Eyes: Can he see? Have him count the number of fingers you display—two or three different numbers. Then question him on some distant object, if possible.

Instruct him to hold his head still. Place your hand approximately 45 cm (18 in.) in front of his face and ask him to follow your hand with his eyes as you move it up and down, then to either side. Confirm that both eyes follow in all directions. Confirm also that his eyes are not deflecting to one side then returning (nystagmus), and the pupils are approximately equal in size.

3. Face: Ask the diver to smile, check that both sides of his face bear the same expression, then ask him to grit his teeth, confirming contracted jaw muscles on either side.

Have the diver close his eyes. Lightly run your finger tips across one side of his forehead; confirm that he senses it. Repeat this on the opposite side and check to be sure the sensation is essentially the same. Continue this at the cheeks and chin.

4. Hearing: Findings will be influenced by surrounding noise levels (check the results against your own hearing). Rub your finger and thumb together adjacent to his ear—have the diver identify this sound. While he keeps his eyes closed, move your hand away and repeat the sound, moving your hand closer until he hears it. Repeat on the other side. Hearing is evaluated continually as you proceed with the evaluation.

5. Shoulders: Ask the diver to shrug his shoulders. Both sides should contract equally. If equipment makes this observation difficult, check for equal muscle tone by pressing down with your hands on both shoulders as he shrugs.

6. Gag reflex: Have the diver swallow, confirm that his Adam's apple moves up and down.

7. Tongue: Ask the diver to stick his tongue out in the middle of his mouth. Confirm that there is no deviation to one side. Check muscle tone.

8. Muscle strength/tone: Confirm that the diver's strength is approximately equal in both arms. Bring his elbows level with his shoulders, hands level with his arms and touching the chest. Ask him to resist as you pull his arms from his chest, push them back, bear down and then up.

Equal leg strength and muscle tone is confirmed by attempting to raise and lower his legs against your resistance.

9. Sensory perception: This should be checked bilaterally by touching lightly as with the face in item 3. Confirming sensation should be apparent and approximately equal at the trunk (moving your hand down), inside and out of the arms and legs. Continue to confirm both sides of one site before moving to a new site. The diver's eyes should be closed during this step; as you move your hand, ask him to confirm the sensation each time you stop.

10. Balance and coordination: Balance and coordination problems may already be apparent. If not, and both space and stability of the platform permit, have the diver stand with feet together. With eyes closed and arms outstretched, he should be expected to maintain his balance. Be prepared to support him should he start to fall.

Confirm coordination by his rapid finger movement from your hand, 45 cm (18 in.) away, to his nose. An alternative test would be for him to run the heel of one foot down the shin of the opposite leg, while supine. Repeat on each side.

Should *any* of the ten steps indicate difficulty or abnormality, central nervous system dysfunction must be suspected.

This completes the basic four minute neurologic exam. Practice it until you have it perfect from memory and teach it to others. It will not only give them a new tool, but will reinforce your own proficiency with the exam.

Remember that every case is different. Tailor your examination to the victim with special emphasis on involved areas and with consideration given to expedience. If a victim complains of pain, numbness, or tingling, test that area particularly for sharp versus dull sensations. (Use objects similar to a safety pin or a cotton swab.)

If any unexplainable abnormalities are noted during this neurological evaluation, air embolism or decompression sickness should be assumed. Keep the victim on 100% oxygen if available and positioned with left side down and legs elevated. Transport the victim to a hyperbaric chamber.

Periodic rechecks, particularly of abnormalities, may show worsening or improvement. Record your findings.

Include this information in a note to accompany the victim listing identifying data, the details of the accident, his dive profiles, symptoms and signs with times of onset, first aid administered, and a log of his breathing and heart rates, periods of unconsciousness, or other medical problems. This will be helpful information for hospital or chamber personnel.

On-site diving accident management flowchart
The following flowchart provides an excellent summary of deck or shore handling of scuba accident victims.

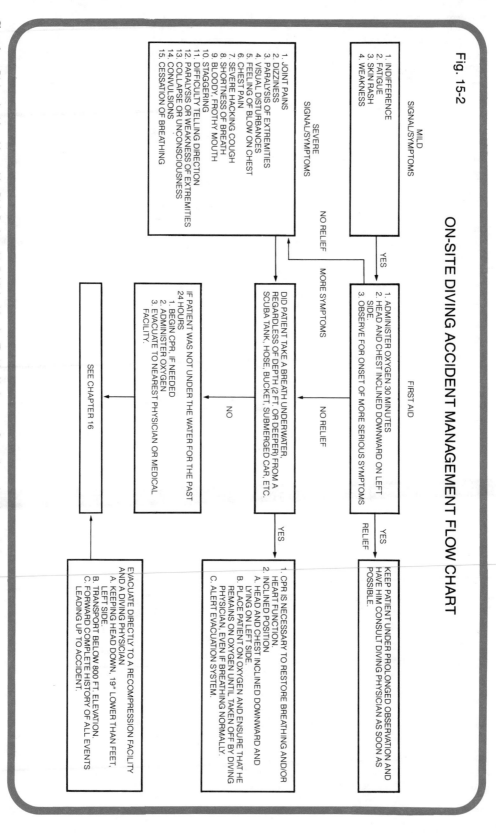

Chart from Diving Accident Manual by Dick Rutkowski. Published by the Florida Underwater Council, used with permission.

Summary

Priorities in emergency care

FIRST PRIORITY is a rapid assessment to detect life threatening disorders of AIRWAY, BREATHING, CIRCULATION and DISABILITY OF NERVOUS SYSTEM.

SECOND PRIORITY is a look, listen and feel assessment of the entire body from head to toe.

GET VICTIM TO EMERGENCY MEDICAL ASSISTANCE AS SOON AS POSSIBLE.

Problems unique to scuba often require recompression in a hyperbaric chamber;

these are:

Air Embolism
Pneumothorax
Mediastinal or Subcutaneous emphysema
Decompression sickness (Bends)

In each case, immediate communication with trained medical personnel is vital to the victim's successful recovery.

Transport to a hyperbaric chamber or hospital

16

As soon as you determine that a victim's condition is serious contact the appropriate agencies.

Communication from a boat

If you are on a boat and there is a marine radio aboard, use the high frequency band, 2182 kilohertz, or the very high frequency band, Channel 16 (156.8 megahertz). The Coast Guard monitors these frequencies continuously. Repeat the word "MAYDAY" to signal an emergency.

Lacking a marine radio, you can use a citizen's band (CB) radio—use the emergency Channel 9, or any other channel. Try to raise someone who can relay your messages. Maintain radio contact for additional messages relayed.

If you have no radio, a nearby boat may have one. Hail it and request the information be relayed. Keep them with you for further contact. Marine law requires assistance to vessels in distress.

Communication from shore

When radio communication is impossible, proceed immediately to the nearest dockage and contact the Coast Guard or other emergency service or agency by telephone.

Other emergency services that may be able to assist include the local harbor patrol, lifeguard service (especially if you were diving near a lifeguarded beach), fire rescue squad, first aid squad, police department, paramedic and ambulance services. Tell them, "This is an emergency!"

Their phone numbers—plus a listing of radio call frequencies, diving physicians, nearby hospitals and recompression chambers—should be recorded on a laminated card and taped to the lid of your first aid kit along with coins for pay phones. In many communities you can dial 911 for emergencies without *any* coin. In addition, remember that telephone operators can usually help you reach an emergency service.

When you reach the emergency service, stay with the phone and do not hang up. Keep the line open for additional communication. If the phone is not near the victim and you cannot move him to the vicinity of the phone, you may need to relay information by shuttling runners or drivers back and forth.

You do not necessarily have to use a *public* phone. Ask a nearby resident or store owner to let you use his place for sheltering the victim and for placing emergency phone calls.

If you are in an isolated area, a car is your most valuable asset. Use it to transport the victim, to go for help, or to make an emergency broadcast over CB radio.

Furnish adequate information

Whether talking over the radio or telephone, speak slowly and distinctly. When excited, most of us tend to talk too fast or to let our emotions make our words unintelligible. In order to assist you, a rescue agency must first understand you. Be sure to furnish sufficient information.

- State that this is an emergency, giving the type of accident and the number of victims.
- If aboard a boat, furnish its name, make and description including identifying features (length, type, colors, cabin, masts, and power). Give its exact location (distance and direction from prominent landmarks), weather, sea conditions, wind direction and boat speed. If calling from land, give your name, the dive location (with directions) and the number of the phone you are using.
- State the condition of the victim. Can he sit up or walk? Is he unconscious or being given CPR? Describe his symptoms and dive history.
- State the type of assistance required.

Where should the victim be taken?

You may not know exactly what you want at this time. But you do know that the victim needs medical assistance urgently. If the victim may have inhaled water, medical care is necessary even if he feels well. He could die hours or days later from the delayed effects of lung damage and low arterial oxygen. If he is suffering from a near-drowning, a wound, a fracture, or a marine life sting, he will require hospital care. But if there is any possibility that bubbles are causing all or part of his trouble, or if he is unconscious following a dive, a hyperbaric chamber is the facility of choice.

The ideal hyperbaric chamber has a double lock, a pressure capability of at least six atmospheres (50 meters or 165 feet of sea water), oxygen breathing equipment and a staff skilled in the treatment of diving accidents. If the closest chamber fails to meet these requirements, consult a diving physician regarding the best procedures.

Emergency calls, collect, to the Diving Alert Network (DAN), 919-684-8111, at the Duke University Medical Center, Durham North Carolina, will be accepted at all hours. Physicians there will share their diving medical expertise and advise proper handling and the availability of nearby hyperbaric chambers. (Divers can join DAN and receive the Diving Accident Manual and Diving Safety Newsletter.)

If aboard a boat, far from shore, you may not be able to consult a diving physician. If there is any doubt about where the victim should go, arrange to transport him to the closest adequately-equipped recompression chamber. Diving physicians there will be able to handle medical problems other than decompression sickness.

When you need a chamber, be sure to call ahead. Chambers are not normally manned around the clock and personnel will usually have to be brought in. Moreover, a series of time-consuming procedures must be implemented to place the chamber in operation. And of course, the chamber may already be committed to another diver. (Many chambers can treat only one patient at a time.)

If space and weight requirements permit, arrange for the victim's buddy to be transported also. He may develop symptoms and need recompression. He can also furnish valuable information regarding the accident and serve as liaison with the victim's family. Be sure the victim is cared for during your communication attempts—especially if he is unconscious.

Transfer of the victim

Before you transfer a victim from a boat or the shore to an aircraft or a vehicle, it will be best to place him on a stretcher. If possible, put a blanket between the stretcher and the victim. Initially, the blanket will insure insulation beneath his body and it can be folded over him for warmth during the transfer. In addition, the victim can be lifted by the

Fig. 16-1

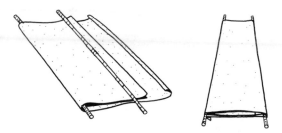

A blanket or rug can be folded over poles so friction holds it in place.

Fig. 16-2

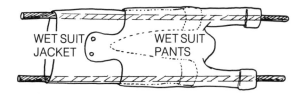

WET SUIT
JACKET

WET SUIT
PANTS

Improvise a stretcher from wet suits or clothes. Use two jackets and pants for a tall victim.

Fig. 16-3

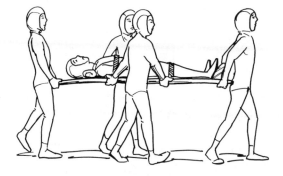

Use four persons to carry a victim, if possible. A surfboard may be used.

blanket out of the stretcher and on to a bed, a table, or a second conveyance.

At least two trained persons, preferably more, should be used in transporting a victim. Use whoever you can get to assist you, but **instruct them in detail** before any actual moving is attempted. If your assistants have any doubt about the procedure, practice beforehand with a volunteer the same size as the victim.

Position the stretcher as close as possible to the victim in order that the lift will be over a short distance. Tell the victim what is happening and what to expect; calm words of reassurance will reduce the chance of shock. Maintain the victim's head lower than his body. Take the victim to the treatment center even if all symptoms disappear.

Almost any board that is long enough and wide enough can be used to carry a victim. A surfboard, paddleboard, door, hatch cover or ordinary plank might do in an emergency. Place a blanket between stretcher and victim for insulation and for ease in lifting him off. Strap him on before lifting and carrying him.

If possible, use four persons to carry a victim, feet first. All four bearers should face the direction of travel—one each at the head and feet and one on each side. The lead man will be able to concentrate on picking the easiest pathway. The one at the head can monitor the victim's condition, watching his face. Commands are given to insure that lifting, carrying and lowering are coordinated.

Accident reporting

You are going to be under considerable emotional stress following any serious accident. You may become obsessed with something careless that was done or with something crucial that was omitted. Avoid blurting it out. Do not blame yourself or anyone else; express no opinions or conclusions. Stick to the facts.

A large crowd may have gathered, drawn by your radio calls or by ambulance sirens. Some bystanders will just gawk. Others will ask questions. Remember, you do not have to talk to anyone. Be courteous, but tell them only enough to enlist their aid if needed, or to keep them from hindering the operation.

Indicate only that there has been a serious accident and that information will be made available once all the facts are compiled.

Local law enforcement officers are entitled to a fuller account. Talk to them in private, away from reporters or bystanders. Answer all questions carefully. Avoid medical or value judgments. Furnish facts, not interpretations.

If there is any possibility that legal action will be taken against you or others, consult an attorney. If you have insurance, alert the agency through which it was obtained. If gear was rented, inform the shop that their equipment figured in an accident. If your employer could be liable, advise him. And of course, you should notify the victim's family and return his belongings (except for dive gear that should be checked).

Especially in the case of a death, the family of the victim desperately wants communication from those involved. Without such contact they are likely to decide that someone did something terribly wrong. A lawsuit may follow. Give them a complete, factual story without interjecting opinions. Tell them the prevention steps that were taken and the rescue procedures employed.

If possible, have an experienced and responsible diver serve as spokesman for your dive group, compiling all relevant facts and answering questions. A spokesman who was not involved in the accident will be more objective. He can serve as liaison with the victim's family and with the diving clubs and shops in the area. He can help to calm emotions and to dispel rumours.

Your job is not over until written reports are completed. Make a list of all witnesses. Get names, addresses and phone numbers. Use the form of the National Underwater Accident Data Center that follows. Have the victim's buddy and all those concerned with the rescue prepare written statements—preferably without consulting each other. Caution them to include only those facts they know from personal experience. Copies of this report are available from the National Underwater Data Center. The form here is not actual size and is included for information only.

UNDERWATER
ACCIDENT REPORT

Forward report to:

NATIONAL UNDERWATER ACCIDENT DATA CENTER

P.O. Box 68 — Kingston, R. I. 02881

VICTIM INFORMATION

Name of Victim: ....
  Last   First   Middle

Address: ....

City .... County .... State ....

Victim's Sex ..... Age ..... Hgt. ...... Wgt. ......

Marital Status: M .... S .... D .... W ... UNK ...

Occupation ....

Employer ....

LOCATION OF ACCIDENT

Location of Accident ....
(use landmarks,
distance from ....
prominent terrain
features. Attach ....
Chart or Map if available)
City .... County .... State ....

CIRCLE LOCATION
(By Code Number)
1. Ocean, Bay, Sea   4. River
2. Minor Lake, Pond, Slough 5. Major Lake, Pond
3. Quarry, Pit, Open Mine   6. Swimming Pool
3A. Cave   7. Great Lakes

TIME AND PLACE OF ACCIDENT

Date and Time of Accident ....
  Day Mo. Yr. Use 24-Hr. Clock

Date and Time of Death ....

Date and Time of Recovery ....

Death Occurred in Water? ....
  (Yes or No)

Autopsy Performed: ....
  (Yes or No)

Cause of Death: ....

Medical Examiner ....
  Name

....
  Address   Phone

CODE FOR NON-FATAL INCIDENT
Circle one only (A, B, C, or D) which best describes seriousness of incident. Important: Report all "incidents", however minor. Describe in detail on page 4. Include equipment factors.

A. Incapacitating injury rendering person unable to perform normal activities as walking or diving or to leave scene without assistance.
B. Nonincapacitating evident injury as loss of blood, abrasions, lump on head, etc.

C. Possible injury indicated by complaining of pain, blackout, limping, nausea, etc.
D. Incident with no apparent injury, (near miss, etc.)

DESCRIPTION OF DIVES AND ACTIVITIES

Description of all dives within previous 12 hours including accident dive.

Depth	Time Down	Surface Interval
....	....	....
....	....	....
....	....	....
....	....	....
....	....	....

Type of Diving: (Explain if Necessary)

Scuba ...... Skin ...... Other ..... Unknown .....

Others in accident ....
  (Yes or No)

Separate report filed ....
  (Yes or No)

At time of incident, Activities engaged in.

Recreational .....
Under instruction .....
Instructing .....
Cave diving .....
Spear fishing .....
Photography .....
Night diving .....
Occupational or Commercial (see back page) .....

At time of incident, Buddy record:

Diving alone .....
Diving with buddy .....
Buddy distance .....
Diving with more than one .....
Distance to next nearest diver .....

Vessels involved ....
  (Yes or No)

U.S. Coast Guard aid sought ....
  (Yes or No)
(Give Details in "Description of Accident", Name, Captain, Address, Phone, etc.)

WITNESSES

Name	Address	Phone	Function/Role
....	....	....	....
....	....	....	....
....	....	....	....
....	....	....	....

* Reported by:

Name ....

Address ....

City .... Phone ....

Other Contacts:

Name ....

Address ....

City .... Phone ....

*If you want to contribute case information and remain "anonymous" please call collect to the Director, John J. McAniff (401) 792-2965. Only Mr. McAniff will accept these calls.

ENVIRONMENTAL CONDITIONS

Sea: Calm .... Moderate .... Rough ....   Weather: Clear .. Cloudy .. Fog .. Snow .. Rain ..

Current: Slight .. Moderate .. Strong .. Direction ...   Thunderstorm .. Tornado, Hurricane .. Other ..

Wave Height: ... Water Depth: ... Type Bottom: ...   Wind Force .... Direction ....

Water Temperature: (°F) ....   Air Temperature: (°F) ....

VISIBLE INJURIES

Illustrate all visible injuries (cuts, abrasions, fractures, etc.)

....

....

....

VISIBLE INJURIES   (Illustrate and describe all visible injuries)

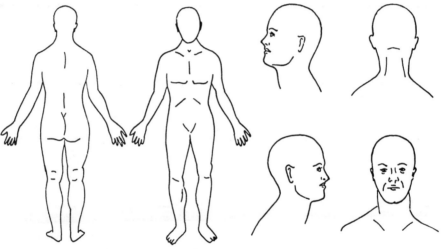

EXPERIENCE DATA

Swimming Experience: Years ......

Skindiving Experience: Years ......

Scuba Experience: Years ......

Courses and Agency

(1) .... Certification Date ....

(2) ....   -DO-   ....

(3) ....   -DO-   ....

HUMAN FACTORS

Hours of sleep in past 24 hours ....

Time of last meal .... What and how much? ....

Time of last alcoholic drink .... What and how much? ....

Any known physical ailments, disability or impairment? ....

....

EQUIPMENT DATA

NOTE: *Equipment Brand, Type and Serial Number data need be included only if malfunction or failure was contributory to the incident.*

Equipment Data Date and Time of Inspection	Brand, Type	Present Before Diving (Yes or No)	Present at Time of Recovery (Yes or No)	Condition	Equipment	Brand, Type, Serial No.	Present Before Diving (Yes or No)	Present at Time of Recovery (Yes or No)	Condition
Diving Suit					Knife (Posit.)				
Hood					Ab Iron				
Boots or Socks					Flashlight				
Gloves or Mits					Depth Gauge				
Mask					Spear Gun				
Snorkel					Compass				
Fins					Regulator				
Weight Belt (lbs.)					Tank				
Buckle					Reserve				
Flotation Device					Watch				
Other Equipment									

For "Occupational" or "Commercial" cases give equipment details on back page.

Flotation Device: Used .... (Yes or No)

Tested after event? .... (Yes or No)

Regulator Tested? .... (Yes or No)

Results ....

Tank: Air Left .... MFG. .... Date .... (PSIG)

Last Hydro-Test Date ....

Last Visual Inspection Date ....

Internal Condition: Clean ....

        Slight Corrosion ....

        Extensive Corrosion ....

By: ....
       NAME   ADDRESS   PHONE

Special Comments on Equipment ....

Equipment Inspected by: ....
       NAME   ADDRESS   PHONE

Equipment: Released to/or Held by: ....
       NAME   ADDRESS   PHONE

DETAILED DESCRIPTION OF ACCIDENT

Describe in detail how the accident happened, including what the person was doing, any specific marine life or objects and the action or movement which led to the event. Include details of first aid or resuscitation efforts. Describe any "Decompression" and/or "Recompression-Treatment" in description of accident.

....
....
....
....
....
....
....
....
....
....
....
....
....
....
....
....
....
....
....
....
....
....
....
....
....

In the instance of an occupational or commercial case please specify category as described below:

COMMERCIAL I (C.I) includes offshore construction and salvage diving, plus oil-and-gas-related operations.

COMMERCIAL II (C.II) includes harbor and inland diving such as construction, shallow pipe inspection, salvage, and repair.

COMMERCIAL III (C.III) includes ship-related diving, such as construction, repair, and hull cleaning.

COMMERCIAL IV (C.IV) includes all types of commercial fisheries, abalone, sea urchin, seaweed harvesting, black coral diving, etc.

COMMERCIAL V (C.V) includes scientific diving for paid consulting purposes.

COMMERCIAL VI (C.VI) includes diving while in training for professional diving.

COMMERCIAL VII (C.VII) includes other types of commercial diving not specifically set forth in the above categories such as underwater photography, private research, commercial treasure diving, archeological diving (and in one instance, a commercial diver acting as a tour guide).

We have listed separately the following categories that are not strictly professional but are occupational in nature:

ACADEMIC (F.) includes scientific research by persons associated with an academic institution.

GOVERNMENT, MILITARY (G.) includes onduty divers in the U.S. Navy, U.S. Army, U.S. Coast Guard, etc.

GOVERNMENT, CIVIL (H.) includes local, state, and federal employees such as police and fire department search and rescue units, etc.

INSTRUCTORS, COMMERCIAL (I.) includes those actively engaged in teaching commercial and professional diving.

INSTRUCTORS, RECREATIONAL (J.) includes certified instructors in sport and recreational diving.

Summary

Should a victim require emergency treatment,

immediate communication to the appropriate authority is vital.
Utilize a radio, telephone or emergency personnel to relay your needs.

Furnish the essential details:

— type of accident
— number of victims
— condition of victim(s)
— location of victim(s)
— type of assistance required

Once the victim is safely in the hands of emergency personnel, complete
an accident report of the facts. Do not write or state items that are
opinion or assumption.

THE AUTHOR

Al Pierce completed his first scuba dive in 1958 on a 60 foot deep wreck in the ocean off Wildwood, New Jersey—no life vest, no reserve, no pressure gauge. Four feet down, his buddy disappeared in a flash, intent on shooting fish. Al blissfully continued to the bottom, entranced by the amazing visibility, the saucer-shaped bubbles, the iridescent jellyfish, the anemone covered wreckage, the swarms of starfish, and the many buck-toothed blackfish feeding on mollusks.

When it became hard to breathe, he reluctantly surfaced. He could have drowned. But he has loved diving ever since.

Al qualified as a YMCA scuba instructor in 1961, as a NAUI instructor in 1968, and as a PADI instructor in 1969. He has trained numerous instructors for these agencies and is also a water safety instructor trainer for the American Red Cross. He received a master's degree from Temple University in 1969 with a thesis on the diving reflex, and has published many articles on scuba safety and rescue. He is an honorary faculty member of Temple University and also teaches at the University of Pennsylvania. He is well known for his award-winning short film, *Deep Water Rescue Breathing* which promotes both mouth-to-mouth and mouth-to-snorkel rescue breathing in open water.

Al's participation in an unsuccessful rescue of a fellow diver convinced him of the urgent need for more and better information, techniques, and training in scuba life saving.

NOTES

NOTES

NOTES

NOTES